A Year in a
B&B in Banff

Praise for *A Year in a B&B in Banff*

"For anyone who ever dreamed of running a B&B, it's a cornucopia of unforgettable characters amidst the beauty of the Canadian Rockies and the fascinating history of Banff. I was glued to the pages. A filmmaker's heaven, it makes you want to be there!"

—Robert M. Johnson
Award-winning producer, *Paper Clips*

A Year in a
B&B in Banff

"I love this town."

JAMIE MACVICAR

AWA

Washington, D.C.

A Year in a B&B in Banff
Copyright 2015 by Jamie MacVicar
First Edition
All rights reserved
MacVicar Enterprises, Inc.

Printed in the United States of America

ISBN 10: 0-692-30272-7
ISBN 13: 978-0-692-30272-9

Library of Congress
Control Number: 2014917588

MacVicar, Jamie F.
   A Year in a B&B in Banff
   Includes bibliography and index.
   Narrative non-fiction / Travel / Satire

Available through www.Amazon.com and book distributors.

Photo and illustration credits are on page 186.

Cover illustration – Jamie Frazer, British Columbia
Design: Susan Beaupre, What If Designs, Leesburg, Virginia

Manufactured by RR Donnelley, Harrisonburg, Virginia
Composition by Coghill Composition Company, Richmond, Virginia

Typeset in Sabon

The imprimatur AWA – Award Winning Authors – Washington, D.C. is granted to the Winners and Finalists of National Literary Awards in the United States. Its artwork is not to be reproduced without the approval of the AWA administrator.

Award Winning Authors
Washington, D.C.

This imprimatur is devoted to the promotion of excellence in the craft of writing.
All of its authors are national literary award recipients.

Winners and Finalists
Pulitzer Prize • National Book Critics Circle Award • PEN Faulkner Award • National Book Award
Nobel Prize for Literature • Marfield Prize-National Award for Arts Writing

Also by Jamie MacVicar

The Advance Man: A Journey Into the World of the Circus

Crossed Pens
with Frederick H. MacVicar and Peter Taylor

for Frederick MacVicar,
who found joy in a Scotsman's sense of humor.

Contents

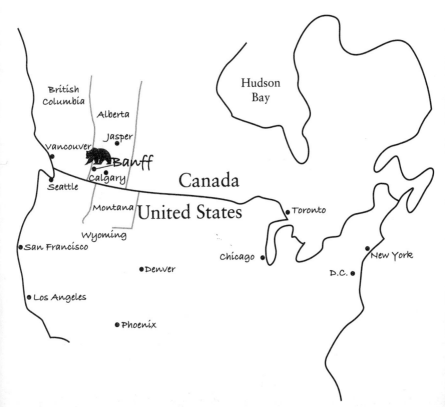

Introduction

The Stoney Indians said they learned how to survive in alpine conditions by studying the wildlife. They cooked over heated stones, inspired perhaps by having observed the big horn sheep spending hours each day licking rocks for purely nutritional value.

In a tiny museum, not far from the Canadian Rockies, a curator had placed the following text on top of an old wood and glass case filled with specimens. Under the watchful eye of a helpful volunteer I wrote it down; for how many of us know a thing about rocks, or for that matter, that what we stand on, and sometimes gaze up at in awe, can be classified into three main types.

Rocks and Minerals

Rocks comprise the entire inorganic, solid portion of the earth. A rock may be formed of a single mineral, but usually rocks are made up of two or more minerals. There are three types of rocks: Sedimentary, Igneous, and Metamorphic.

Sedimentary Rock

The word sedimentary means "material formed by water, wind, or glacier." All rocks disintegrate slowly by weathering. Particles of clay, silt, sand, and gravel travel to new locations through water, wind, and ice.

These relocated particles eventually become cemented together as "clastic" sedimentary rocks. *Clastic* sedimentary rocks are conglomerates (fashioned from granules such as gravel), sandstone (created from sand), siltstone and mudstone (formed from silt), and shale and claystone (formed from clay).

Chemical sedimentary rocks are salt, gypsum, limestone, dolomite, borates, nitrates, and phosphates.

Igneous Rock

Igneous means "from fire." Igneous rocks are formed by the cooling and hardening of magma, a molten substance inside the earth.

Intrusive Igneous Rocks, or "plutonic" rocks, crystallize from magma that cools and hardens within the earth, surrounded by preexisting rock, known as "country" rock (sandstone, limestone, and shale). This magma cools slowly, creating course-grained rock.

Extrusive Igneous Rocks, or "volcanic" rocks, are formed at the surface of the earth as a result of volcanic activity. Molten lava flowing from a volcano cools and crystallizes rapidly, forming fine-grained rock.

Metamorphic Rock

Metamorphic means "changed." Metamorphic rocks are changed deep beneath the earth's surface by the great stresses and high pressures and temperatures of mountain building, or when magma intrudes into rock.

With such increasing temperatures and pressure:
- Shale changes to slate, to phyllite, to schist, and finally to gneiss.
- Sandstone changes to quartzite.
- Limestone changes to marble.
- Basalt changes to schist, and then to amphimolite.
- Granite changes to gneiss.
- Coal changes to peat, to lignite, to bituminous, to anthracite.

Perhaps all of this was more than either you or I ever wanted to know about rocks, but this is a story, after all, about a year in the Canadian Rockies . . . and I suspected that deep down you wanted to know.

*Text courtesy of the Hutson Museum.

Chapter 1

"...and I also own a small B&B."

Suddenly transported to another place, one can't shake the memories of home. You step onto a country road and for a moment wonder, where's all the rushing traffic? Or you round the corner past a tenement and expect an onslaught of smells that aren't there. For me it's shit. I stop and stare at it. I'm amazed by it. Is it wolf shit, bear shit, coyote or wolverine? No, you idiot, it's dog shit. You're on the streets of Paris. And it's everywhere!

For a modern day urbanite, wildlife tracking hadn't been on my list of must learns. Yet it wasn't long before I knew that a print in the snow with two nail marks belonged to the dog family, including a wolf and coyote. The same print, slightly rounder with no nail marks, signaled a cat; a bobcat, lynx, or cougar retracting their claws as they do when they walk. Diagonal versus registered, one print stepping into another, further clarified any guesses. And what is fascinating are the signs of wildlife activity: a wolf track next to a deer hoof, and then another wolf track ten yards away, and then another. Could utter fear match a pack's cunning chase?

I'd taken a course in tracking not long after arriving in Banff. It was taught by a professional tracker.

Clueless, I asked, "Who hire's a professional tracker?"

"The local governments, sometimes," he said. "If the environmentalists protest enough, the government will ask for a study of wildlife movement before green lighting a new development."

"Does it stop the development?"

"No, unfortunately the developers usually win in the end. Wildlife corridors have often become whatever's left." He paused for a moment. "Luckily thousands of square miles in the Canadian Rockies have been removed from the threat of political indifference and greed."

But back to shit, or scat as it's known to excrement enthusiasts. A careful study of it examines the size, the shape, the color and tapering. And whether or not it contains grass, ants, berries, small bones, or hair. And if it's large, very large, most important of all, is it *fresh*? And I mean, is it steaming fresh?

Because coming upon steaming fresh bear shit is a plan alterer every time!

Naturally, we keep extra cans of bear spray at the Bed and Breakfast for our guests. As I mention this to our new arrivals, and fear creeps over their faces, I try to lighten the mood. "There's nothing to worry about. Take Ol' Uncle Ned. He was mauled by a grizzly last spring, and he's already off life support and learning to communicate by blinking!"

When the nervous laughter subsides I carefully explain with Canadian patience how to use the spray. "It's a very strong pepper spray, and it flies out like a shot. It will easily go thirty feet against the strongest wind. Just aim for the face. And don't miss. It's the best deterrent there is."

"Making noise," I add, "not with bells that block your sensory awareness, but with loud conversation to eliminate a surprise encounter, helps assure you will never have to employ it."

"Have you ever had to use it?" a guest will frequently ask.

And it's here that the American side of me, for I was born in Alaska to Canadian parents, resists the urge to reply, "No, I never have. I just hold it up and say 'Well grizzly, you're probably wondering if this can holds one blast or two. Do you feel lucky? Well, do ya?'"

So how did this half-American, half-Canadian from Virginia end up in the Canadian Rockies in a charming B&B in Banff? A woman, of course...and what a beautiful woman. Like those with true beauty she has multiple looks, from attractive to comfortably plain. But often enough, with a turn of the head, a beauty transpires that would weaken a mortal man, left stunned by the awareness he had nothing to do with creating it.

"Connie, what brings you to Mexico?" I asked.

"I needed a small vacation."

"What do you do?"

"I'm a teacher," she said. "I teach grade three." And then her eyes shimmered with pride. "And I also own a small B&B."

It was a few months later that I arrived in Banff, a storybook town nestled in Bow Valley in the Canadian Rockies. I walked up the flagstone path, past a colorful sign that read 'Banff Avenue B&B.' And I knocked on the door to this red cedar home sheltered among the trees.

———·———

So this is a love story, about a woman, two countries, and a B&B. And, oh yes, as much as I hate to end this chapter on a discordant note, lest I forget, there was also a small red and white sign in the window. "For Sale."

Chapter 2
Canadians Invented the Queue

I don't think we're in Kansas anymore Toto. I ambled toward an intersection and eyed a dozen Canadians standing amiably, obediently, on opposite corners under a "Don't Walk" sign . . . without a car in sight!

Later that week I borrowed Connie's car. I came to a stop sign and began to examine a local map, only to discover I'd lost track of time and three cars behind me had been waiting patiently for the past five minutes. And no one had honked!

Who are these people? Why am I not lying bleeding by the side of the road?

The fact is, Canadians are rule-abiding, well-mannered, and just plain nice. An American opined, "they look like us, but there's something different about them. Something a bit odd."

Even when they're not nice, they're nice. To say one just caught a polite young man peeing on your house would generally be labeled a non-sequitur. But indeed we did, and inebriated as he was, I expected a "Fuck you!" in reply to my "What the hell are you doing?" But instead he hollered back, "I'm sorry. I'm so sorry!"

I read later with amusement that a small town on Prince Edward Island built a round-a-bout only to create a fiasco. The townspeople had to be gathered and told to stop being so considerate. Each driver froze at the circle. "You go. No, you go. No please, you go."

In fact, I became convinced Canadians invented the queue when later, with my eyes still blurry from an overnight flight to Heathrow, I searched for my gate amidst the usual airport mayhem and disarray. Like a mirage it loomed before me, eighty passengers standing perfectly in line, all nice and orderly, and I knew from a far distance that I'd found it: Air Canada.

Yet despite a ubiquitous respect for law and order, it seems to be trumped in their judicial system by kindness. To an American it's startling to see the disparity in punishment. Often for what a U.S. offender receives a ten-year sentence, in Canada the criminal is awarded with a suspended sentence and community service. "Aw, e's a good lad. Ah'm sure e won't do it again," I can almost hear the judge saying.

Though leniency and forgiveness in the hope that human lessons are learned is admirable, sometimes it's downright absurd. In one case I observed, a cardiologist who stabbed his two small children to death after discovering his wife was having an affair was acquitted of murder on the grounds he'd been depressed.

Reading the news this morning (I couldn't make this up if I tried), under the headline "Drug Courier Spared Jail Time," the local paper states, "Louis Berry entered his plea to possession for the purpose of trafficking" (he had 12 pounds of the stuff!) "in front of Judge Marlene Graham. Graham agreed to a conditional sentence. 'I think you've had quite a wakeup call by this event,'" Graham said. In the U.S. the judge would have said, "You're going to jail and *that* will be your wakeup call!"

Astonishing as well is the case of Conrad Black, an unrepentant malfeasant if ever there was, (though America might gladly keep him in exchange for Donald Trump). A former Canadian newspaper baron, Black is serving a seven-year sentence in the U.S. for bilking his shareholders and trying to hide the evidence. Yet, he's a featured columnist in Canada's national newspaper, the *National Post*. An American visitor wrote, "Do what you want with your own judicial system, but don't make a mockery of ours!"

But if it isn't fear of Draconian punishment, what is it that makes most Canadians so law abiding, to the point of adhering to "Don't Walk" signs with nary a car in sight? And why are Canadians so naturally polite, so that *Please* and *Thank you* and *Excuse me* are a part of their national character?

Some have said that Canadians took the best from Britain and the best from America and discarded the rest. But to me the answer lies closer to their parenting.

Canadian parents don't see their offspring as little people whose favor needs to be curried, but as children who need to be taught what's proper, and right from wrong. Love and play are just as easily mingled with a stern admonishment, "all elbows on the table shall be carved."

———·———

Connie was the type of woman who didn't talk about her feelings. But she also couldn't hide how she felt. Though how she felt wasn't always readily seen. You had to look for it. You had to be observant.

It was springtime in Banff and the rivers and streams had begun to flow with the glacial run-off. A few orange and purple perennials poked their heads up in Connie's garden.

Connie and I sat at ease on the back deck. The inside of the house was immaculate, but I couldn't help noticing that the outside was in need of repair. A barbeque pit had accumulated windblown leaves. A five-foot cedar fence hadn't been stained in years. And beyond the green grass, beside a garage that resembled a small country barn, I could see junk had been allowed to pile up: planks of old wood amidst a rusted fender or two.

"How long have you had the B&B?" I asked.

"It's been four years now," she said.

"Was it something you always wanted to do?"

"Not really," she laughed. "As a teacher I was searching for something to do in the summer. We looked at four or five houses, but this home seemed ideal. Then I lived in dust for a year as new plumbing and bathrooms were installed."

"Did your husband enjoy the B&B?"

"He helped, but he didn't take much of an interest. I've been doing the best I can."

The sun that had been toasting the deck slipped between a mountain peak and the branches of a backyard tree. I was still unsettled by the "For Sale" sign, on the one hand innocuous and hardly noticeable, and on the other hand threatening, sooner or later upending a dream Connie had so thoughtfully nourished.

"Is that why the house is for sale?"

"The upkeep is a part of it, I suppose. But I don't really have much choice. After almost two years the divorce is now final. And the house will have to be put up for sale."

It seemed as though, for the moment, Connie had put her feelings away in a box, choosing to not think about it, in a slow real estate market that hadn't produced any interest.

Chapter 3
A Mystery Solved . . . the Origins of Banff Avenue B&B

How many of us, long after we're gone, live on through our passion? For many, that pride takes the form of their children. For others it may be found in their work. But for others, often artists, writers, or sculptors, like Michelangelo and David, their passion arouses more than admiration and curiosity. It makes us want to know more, much more, about who created the art.

Built in 1955 Connie's B&B sits on a cozy corner spot on Banff Avenue, one of only four single-family homes left on Banff's famous street. Its front windows offer guests stunning views of Norquay and Cascade mountains. Observers would say it's an "ordinary home," and they would be right, except for one salient feature. If they opened the front door, to their left, past the windows and wing-backed chairs, they would be greeted by an impressive stone fireplace.

And this is no ordinary fireplace. Rising from floor to ceiling it is plain to see that each and every stone had been carefully selected over a lifetime, stones mortared above and below a Rundle rock mantle, with patience and craftsmanship. Stones with stripes, some with fossils, quartz and crystal, are nestled beside prehistoric club heads. Smooth green surfaces the color of jade join a palette of rich, warm hues from burnt orange to Swiss coffee. One of the stones has an image in the shape of a duck, another in the contours of Africa. Every stone is distinct, from a size that would fit into your pocket to others weighing thirty pounds or more.

And what is amazing, what the visitor wouldn't see, is that downstairs beneath the living room, under the top floor fireplace, is a second stone fireplace with rocks just as exquisite and rare. This was clearly a work of passion. But who was it, I wondered, that laboriously collected these stones? And why? Was it a knowledgeable geologist or just a lover of natural beauty? Where were the stones found? And when? And from the number and sizes of the rocks, how did he or she carry them here? And what about the old wrought iron screen in front of the fireplace with the letter P on top and the initials P, J, J, G welded on the bottom? What did the letters represent?

By coincidence, we were soon to find out. And the answers would, surprisingly enough, reveal a man well-known to Banff, that through his passion, lives on through the stone fireplace.

But there are two other pieces to the story, parts to the puzzle that had peaked my curiosity as much as the fireplace. On the back corner of the lot, in a shaded spot that evokes a small town tranquility, stands a tall spruce tree. Lazily wandering nearby, breathing in the tree's sweet smell, I looked up and discovered a rusted bicycle rim, twenty feet up, now embedded in the bark through the passage of time. How fascinating, I thought; it's a pulley that carried a line to the house that stood on the property before Connie's home was built. Like the stone fireplace, I would gaze at it and be pulled back in time.

The second curiosity was the *spirit* that resided in the house. A short time after arriving, while down in the washroom, I heard footsteps walking around the upstairs entrance. The sounds were so clear I called out to see who was there. But I was the only one home, and all the doors to the house were locked. Connie expressed surprise, but then experienced the exact phenomenon a few weeks later. Laughingly, she said, "I've from time to time smelled pipe tobacco wafting pleasantly through the house."

But whose treasure, if not a *magnum opus*, lives on in the home. . . . the person who so carefully transported the many stones. . . . the same person who many years ago attached a bicycle rim to a then much smaller tree? Updating her B&B license, having no idea when the home might sell, Connie walked into the office of the Parks Administration building. "Out of curiosity," she said to the attendant, "would your records identify the original property owner?"

He pulled out an old document, and then paused, "Well, I'll be. The original leaseholder was Ebenezer William Peyto, better known as Bill Peyto. It appears he leased the property, with no improvements, in 1907. And then he built a home there, where he lived until he died in 1943 at the age of seventy four."

A local legend, this was the same Bill Peyto whose arresting visage graces the entrance signs welcoming modern-day tourists to Banff, with an expression of certitude amidst the confusion felt by the new arrivals. As surprised as the attendant, Connie asked, "What happened to the house and property?"

He glanced at the records. "His estate was managed by his brother Walter whose son Stan Peyto, then purchased the property. Apparently Stan and his wife Inez moved into Bill's house, and in 1955 they tore down the dwelling and built the present home that you now occupy. It appears that Stan and Inez lived in the home for thirty years."

"Is there a photograph of Bill's house?" Connie asked.

"I don't know, but if there is, the archives might have it."

A few days later Connie and I strolled into the Whyte Museum archives office. "There should be a photo," said the archivist. "In

1937 the local government, in fear it wasn't collecting all of the taxes from cabin rentals, went around and took a photo of every house in Banff, and more often than not, of the backyards."

A large diagram on a table indicated a block and lot number for every house in Banff. "I'll retrieve the files," she said. "Please slip on the white gloves in the box before handling the photos."

A few minutes later, under the glow of a small lamp, we found ourselves staring at the front of Bill Peyto's home. Sure enough, its roof in relation to Tunnel Mountain's skyline was identical to ours. As I studied the photo, looking for other similarities, I thought about the homes that had come and gone in Banff that, other than an unintended 1937chronicle, had little record of their history at all.

But who is Bill Peyto? As so often happens with iconic images, whether it's the "showman" P.T. Barnum or the "humourist" Mark Twain, or in this case the handsome steely-eyed "mountain man" Bill Peyto, their complexities are slowly stripped away.

And it's the thrill of biography, as writer Ted Hart accomplishes in *Bill Peyto's Mountain Journal*, to reach behind the surface for a glimpse of who they really were. Yes, Bill Peyto was a loner. Yes, he was a prospector, having staked a claim, and, yes, he was an entrepreneur and mountain guide, which he parlayed into years as one of the National Park's wardens. But what most people don't know, what isn't as easily seen in his rugged photograph, is that Bill Peyto was also a scholar.

He was fascinated with paleontology and geology and immersed himself in the books of his time on the subject. Quoting from Ted Hart's fictionalized yet studied account of his activities Bill Peyto can be heard saying, "There's a nice green meadow with interesting quartz outcroppings in the limestone," or "My time poking around the rocks has been productive. I've gathered samples, some containing copper from the lakes at the foot of Healy Pass," or "it's here near Emerald Lake in a fossil bed that I picked up my first sample of Cambrian Trilobite." And further on, Hart relays Bill Peyto's excitement "finding invertebrate fossils embossed in the rock," and how "quickly he got out his hammer to chip some loose."

Bill Peyto chose not to have many close friends. But he relished the company of one man who shared his interest for fossils and minerals and his findings of prehistoric clubs and arrowheads. It was Norman Sanson, the well-known Banff museum curator and weather recorder. Together they went on collecting expeditions around Lake Minnewanka and hidden areas known only to a few.

And though I could be wrong, if I needed any further evidence that it was Bill Peyto who passionately collected the rocks now beautifying the B&B's fireplaces, it was the tiny script I discovered on one of the stones that was inscribed "Sanson-1887."

But if Bill Peyto carried these rocks out on horseback to his home on Banff Avenue, who built the two fireplaces? Did his nephew Stan and his wife Inez design them, employing Bill's collection no doubt stored in his sheds, or when they razed Bill's house in 1955 did they somehow build around two fireplaces that had already been vertically constructed?

"We'll have to ask Inez," Connie said. And though Stan had passed away in 1984, Inez, now ninety years old, still resided in the Bow Valley.

"I'd be delighted to drive over for tea. I'm so happy you are interested!" Inez replied to our invitation.

A neighbor, Bob Edwards (known as "Sharkey" in his younger years for his hockey prowess), who has lived in a home behind Connie's during his eighty some years, remembered Inez well. "She's one of the nicest people you will ever meet." Bob Edwards also remembered Bill Peyto. Smiling, he said, "He'd ride up Beaver Street on his way home, and we'd run and hide because he'd shoo us away for playing in the street."

I suspected the children had exaggerated their fears. Bill's brother, Walter, lived diagonally across the street, where the Shell station now stands, and Bill enjoyed the company of Walter's six children, carving wooden toys and telling stories for their wide-eyed pleasure.

—·—

Inez had an ageless beauty, mirrored by an infectious enthusiasm and girlish charm. And if ninety years had brought its hardships she was disinclined to show it. Inez arrived accompanied by her son Paul's wife, Susan, who, like Inez, had a pioneering feminine toughness.

As soon as Inez and Susan strolled in the door, Inez exclaimed, "There's the fireplace," and she walked over with pride for a closer look. Inez took a seat in a comfortable chair. "My son Paul made the wrought iron screen. That's P for Peyto on top and the initials of my four children, Paul, Jimmy, Judy and Gordon along the bottom." Wistfully, she added, " It's so wonderful the home is still here. It's the last Peyto home still standing in Banff."

While Connie brought out the tea, I asked "Can you tell us about the fireplace?"

"Stan and I had it built when we constructed the house."

"Where did all the incredible rocks come from?"

"The whole family collected them. Stan never went anywhere without his backpack. Often we would find them in creek beds, where water and time had enriched their color. Over years of family outings we selected them, some by a stream half-way to Radium, some near Bow Lake by Dolomite Mountain, and others in the Cascade valley. And, of course, quite a few were from uncle Bill's collection of specimens."

Susan remarked, "My husband Paul is just like his great uncle Bill. He's happy spending days alone in the back country. And he's always returning with exotic stones and artful pieces of wood."

As Inez reflected on her family, I couldn't help thinking how remarkable it is that Bill's fascination with geology had been shared by Stan and Inez, and now through another generation of Peytos . . . a similar appreciation lives on.

"Do you remember much about Bill Peyto?"

"What you saw was what you got!" Inez laughed. "He was a handsome man. You knew when he walked into a room that this was somebody special." I surmised he had what today we call, *presence*. It emanated, I suspected, from knowing exactly who he was, what he valued, and what he enjoyed, which was more often than not being left alone among the natural wonders—the rocks and minerals, wildlife and fauna, in the back country of the Canadian Rockies.

There was a moment of silence. "But Bill," Inez said, "was always a perfect gentleman." And then she added an anecdote that was telling. "Walter's wife, we called her grandma Peyto, baked delicious homemade bread, but she'd purposely burn one of the loaves for Bill. That's the way he liked it." And suddenly, the image of Bill, the lone trapper and guide, was softened by a matronly woman who looked upon him with love and regard.

"Do you think Bill Peyto would have enjoyed the notoriety he's received?" I asked.

"No, I don't think so," Inez replied. And I remembered something poignant from Ted Hart's account. If I'm going to be famous for anything, Bill Peyto had said, I'd rather it was for the discovery of something scientifically important, perhaps a new fossilized species embedded in a stone.

———•———

Combing through the archives there was one other photo I discovered. It was a photo of Bill Peyto with his wife Ethel, much later in life, standing happily it appears on the back stoop of their house. Unseen in front of them, about sixty feet away, stands a sturdy still growing spruce tree. And above them is the other end of the pulley that had pulled me back in time.

Chapter 4
The U-Back Café

"You say you live in Poof?" I had teased.

"No, Banff."

A young man at our table in the Mexican resort kindly tutored me, "Banff is the Aspen of Canada. It's known for its world-class skiing."

Though I was well traveled, I'd actually never heard of it. From Europe to the Middle East and Asia to South America, almost four million visitors come through the park gates each year. But Banff's tourism department hadn't publicized Banff much in the States. (Big mistake. Canada's currency is colored. Americans would just think of it as funny money. You could steal them blind!)

Aspen aside, arriving for the first time, I still had a mental picture of a fishing camp in the middle of the boonies. So as the shuttle bus from the airport turned off the highway for its final stretch into Banff I was surprised to see glittery white lights illuminating a string of fancy hotels . . . and gone was my vision of Connie cleaning trout for the local lumberjacks and their wives.

But this was the shoulder season, when the local population of seventy eight hundred reclaimed the community. And what made Banff special was behind those glitzy hotels was a Norman Rockwellian town of kids pushing to school on their scooters while the inhabitants, acclimated to the alpine weather, dressed comfortably in jeans and flannel shirts.

And what helped to keep it this way was a unique and little known fact. The town isn't allowed to grow. The reason is that Banff, unlike almost any resort town in the world, is located inside a national park. As a result, beyond its tiny circle—you can stroll from one end to the other in twenty minutes—the town by legal statute isn't permitted to expand. That means *no* urban sprawl, *no* chalets creeping up the side of mountains, and most important of all, within a five-minute drive in any direction you're in the middle of a vast, unspoiled wilderness.

There is also a cap on commercial space, and its population density can't exceed ten thousand residents. But the most valuable and sensible restraint, a restriction that has helped to preserve its character, is the "Need to Reside" law. You cannot buy a house in Banff unless you work full-time in the town, and that includes King Faruk and the Hollywood A list. The motive is simple. Without this restriction the houses would be bought up by the wealthy, the prices would soar, and soon after, the teachers and firemen, storekeepers and wardens couldn't afford to live in their own community.

For years the parks service, Parks Canada, had run the town with the Parks Superintendant acting as the municipal authority, but in the late 1980s the town was given its own management charter with an elected town council and mayor. "We just weren't that good at it," said a park official. "Given a choice between building a trail in the back country and a new city sewer line, we'd take the new trail every time."

That doesn't mean Parks Canada doesn't still rule with an iron hand, for it was they who imposed the restrictions. The town land is owned by the government, and any activity that might impinge on the wildlife or area must be approved by disinclined park officials.

None of this stifles conflict. For like all resort towns a battle constantly rages between the developers who naturally see ripe opportunities, and the preservationists who, like Connie and I, would never allow anything demolished. It's the reason a Banff former mayor was elected by acclamation. Nobody else wanted the job!

Perhaps Connie's passion reflects what she values, for before fancy hotels replaced the quaint motels, there were nicely built cabins—some still standing—behind many of the local's homes. And it wasn't unusual for them to rent out a room or two. Banff started as a tourist town. And for Connie, I suppose, the heart of its accommodations will always be the B&B.

———•———

Connie and I grew closer, and I'd begun to fly back and forth. Soon forth got better then back, and fortunately I had the flexibility. For twenty-five years I had run a graphic design and communications firm in Washington, D.C. But I'd promised myself that if I had saved enough money by the age of fifty I'd be done. Twenty-five years running a business was long enough. There were other things I wanted to do. Chief among them, see the world, and finish writing a book, *The Advance Man: A Journey Into the World of the Circus*, about my experience as an advance man for Ringling Bros. and Barnum & Bailey Circus.

But the cities of the world hadn't prepared me for the foibles of small town life. Oh, what I didn't know.

Fudge and sweaters seemed to form the backbone of Banff's retail economy, along with the charm of the corner café. And Connie and

I had a favorite café. It sat near the bridge on the edge of town with a window view overlooking the river.

It was Sunday afternoon. I was in a relaxed mood. "Let's take the paper and wander down to the café."

It was half-past four when we arrived. We pulled up two stools and ordered a cup of coffee. But no sooner had we sat down than a young waitress began vacuuming the floor. And what's more, she began stacking the chairs. I looked at the clock. The café didn't close until five o'clock. I glared at the waitress to no avail.

"We walked all the way down here to quietly read the paper," I finally said.

"Sorry about that," she said, as the industrial vacuum roared even closer.

Incensed, and unable to restrain myself any longer, I blurted out, "Who owns this place?"

"She does," she said, and she pointed at a little Asian woman behind the counter.

I got up, not noticing Connie had quietly slipped out the door, and approached her. "You're still open for thirty more minutes. Do you realize how annoying this is?"

"I am sorry. I do this every day!"

"Then that makes you the worst business in Banff!" I exclaimed, and I stormed out the door.

Connie was waiting outside. "The nerve of her," I said.

Well, all was fine and good, and I'd said my piece, except for one thing. I'd also talked myself out of my favorite café.

Some weeks later, Connie and I were walking downtown. I asked, "On a scale of one to ten what are the odds she's forgotten me?"

"A twelve," Connie retorted. "This is a tourist town. She sees a hundred faces a day!"

I opened the door. I looked at her . . . she looked at me . . . then she pointed her finger. "You back!"

———•———

And from that moment on we've called it the U-Back Café. I walked up to the owner. I smiled. She smiled back.

"Do you still start vacuuming before you close?"

"Every day!"

And from then on, we arrived before four o'clock.

———•———

But at least there was more than one café. For like most small towns there are a multitude of monopolies; one hardware store, one office supply store, one car wash, and, for that matter, not many landscapers either.

"I'll call Luke," Connie said.

I had begun to clean out the back corner, where, under the rusted car parts, there was an old sled and more piles of rotten wood. It was directly under the spruce tree where Bill Peyto had strategically placed the bicycle rim pulley. "My ex-husband seldom threw anything away," Connie said.

Like any smart business, Connie reserved ten percent of the annual revenues to put back into the B&B. And this was an eyesore. Making it attractive would only add to the home's salability.

Luke showed up, wiry and fidgety.

"We'd like to take the corner fence down, lay in new grass, and put a nice mulch cover around the tree. Can you give me a complete estimate?"

"No problem," Luke replied, and he scratched out the number $1,700 on a pocket-sized pad of paper.

"Will that do it?" I asked.

"You bet!"

Luke did indeed do a fine job. And then he sent us a bill. $2,100.

I asked Luke to come over. "What's this?" I inquired. "Your bill is $400 over your estimate."

Luke pulled out his crumpled pad. "The extra $400 is for the grass. You didn't think that was included did ya? That *would* be a heck of a deal!"

I looked over at Connie, and nodded, biting my lip. Had I not learned my lesson? We might need him again.

———•———

Real estate was slow, and hardly anyone had come by to look at the house. "I couldn't move out until the end of the summer anyway," Connie said, sounding relieved, "I'm already filling up with bookings."

More worrisome still, there were twenty three nights sold for May, and double that for June. Connie's school year didn't end until June 30th.

Connie already looked tired. I looked around at the unkempt yard and the unpainted fence. "I only know how to make two kinds of eggs, scrambled and very scrambled. What would you think about my flying back to Washington, and then driving up for the whole summer?"

As though nothing I could have said would have sounded any better, she quietly replied, "I'd like that."

———•———

I'd never driven across the country. I savored the thought of my old Celica convertible. Thirty five hundred miles . . . eight or so days ought to do it.

Chapter 5

"Where are you from? I'm glad you asked . . . Wyoming."

I had learned, after a few years of serious travel, that if you have one solid month there is nowhere in the world you can't go. South Africa, Istanbul, the Far East, you name it . . . thirty days is enough for one hell of a journey.

But four months away requires more planning. We live in a world of minutia. To stay "official" takes an inordinate amount of time. There are forms to be filled out, things to be renewed, things that expire (even my bank ATM card has an expiration date—what's that about?). Deserted on a tropical island? Try it for three months. Your life will have been repossessed!

I called Bonnie, a part-time assistant, an administrative luxury I had kept. She agreed to collect my mail, pay my bills, and water the house plants once a week. I pre-wrote four months of checks for her, and then I wracked my brain for anything else I might have forgotten.

The lack of time for distant travel was the primary reason I'd closed the design firm. One or two weeks doesn't do it. Nor does it work for most Americans in general. Understandably, beyond

Europe, Mexico or the Caribbean, I could count the number of Americans traveling solo I had met on one hand; French, Germans, and Italians, but rarely Americans. So it didn't surprise me to read that only five percent of Americans own a passport, and of those that do and travel abroad, eighty percent of their travel is to Mexican and Caribbean resorts.

Other countries, I've noticed, promote gap years; a year in which young people between high school and college are encouraged to explore the globe, often by backpack while lodging at affordable hostels. European employers value this experience when considering applicants, in some cases viewing it as more educational than sitting in a classroom earning a questionable advanced degree.

So who could fault me, I figured, for taking a gap decade to happily make up for lost time. *The Advance Man: A Journey Into the World of the Circus*, a seventeen-year project, had finally been published. I loaded three cases of books into the car for publicity purposes and guests of the B&B. Then I squeezed in my suitcase, closing the lid, with barely a glance back at the front door.

———•———

Travel—a new trip—God I love it! Isn't it the lack of minutia and the freedom from phones, emails, and all the rest of it, I reflected, at the heart of my love for travel? It's the freedom to observe, to get lost in my own thoughts, to simply live, untethered from all the distractions that interfere with our ability to engage all our senses.

Or perhaps because we're surrounded by the familiar, most of our thoughts are about the past and the future. Travel rivets you to the here and now, while sometimes merging the past with the present.

I glanced at the map. If I could make it to Columbus, Ohio that would be a good first day. Three hours out of Washington I stopped for gas on the outskirts of a small town. Around the curve I could see a village of neatly trimmed lawns, old homes with porch swings and back yard gardens. I followed an urge to drive among the tree-lined streets, slowing to gaze at verandahs, while noticing a sidewalk lifted by a large oak tree.

I'm not sure what I hoped to see, perhaps a milk truck filled with empty bottles, or elderly men in button-down sweaters, vestiges of a time long gone. More likely I was in search of a warm feeling, a moment of looking again through the eyes of a child, loved by people who lived in a world that seemed to make sense to them.

As the day went on, the rolling farm fields of Pennsylvania turned into the wooded hollows of West Virginia. Outside Wheeling I crossed a bridge high above a brown, muddy river. Smoke stacks from a dilapidated power plant rose out of the bluff on the western bank.

I looked over at the approaching city. The homes were old, but they weren't the pristine, old homes I'd seen earlier. These houses looked tired; two-storied wooden and slate-tiled structures that probably never looked shiny and new. This was clearly a blue collar town built on the back of a fading manufacturing base.

People often think of the States as politically divided while rarely pondering how separate are its white and blue collar classes. Our paths rarely cross, and when they have, and I have tried to connect, as they have with me, we've quickly run aground in the search for common interests. It's as frustrating as speaking to a foreigner when you only know their language on a first-grade level. I don't know how to hunt anything, catch anything, or fix anything. In point of fact, I am far more interested in "why" than "how."

"Why do you suppose it took fifty thousand years for mankind to put wheels on the bottom of suitcases?"

Who cares was the look that would cross my ex-father-in-law's face. "Are you going to fetch me the pliers or not so that I can show you how to change your lawn mower's oil?"

I used to think they looked up to us college educated types. But they don't. They see us as manipulators, sizing up the shot, playing the angles. And they see it impacting their lives—in fees that don't make sense, insurance policies that don't really pay, pensions that somehow disappear, and jobs that get taken away to maximize the profits for a hedge fund magnate.

Theirs is a world where character comes into play—courage, loyalty, physical strength, and resilience in the face of adversity. It's not executives, they note, rushing into the burning World Trade Center Tower, nor the Congressman's son fighting alongside them in Afghanistan.

They simply don't trust us. And, frankly, neither do I.

Maybe it's harder than ever to live in a world of old rules versus new. For it seems as though many in the working class are in and out of avoidable trouble. In the modern-day world, if you don't think three moves ahead, or you don't stay on top of the endless minutia, or react too impulsively, your life can suddenly get stressful; you can find yourself in a bucketful of hurt.

But in one sense, perhaps more than others, I had grown to admire them. It was why I hadn't given up trying to find a connection. And it was why I found their women increasingly sexy. When they walked down the street and swiveled their hips, they did so with *authenticity*.

Day two.

Who ever thought it would look like this? I'd pulled out of Zanesville, Ohio at 6 A.M., and I could see a nice pattern emerge. Go to bed early, then start at dawn to see farm houses and fields slowly take shape in the mist.

But that was then, and I'd been driving for three hours, and I was mired in a sea of noisy traffic. My scenery was a swamp of square buildings, chain stores, and fast food restaurants. Miles and miles of architectural default. Take down the Home Depot sign and put up the Walmart logo. Would anyone really notice?

From Chicago eastward it seemed as though the interstate landscape had been devoured by urban sprawl. I guess this was nothing new, but time out West had changed my perspective . . . ugly was no way to live.

But what was sadder still was the family owned businesses that had disappeared. Gone were Smith's Hardware Store, Al's Grocery, and Bill's Appliance Repair, and vanishing fast were the small motels and local restaurants, unable to compete with the standardized fare.

It used to be that small business was the backbone of the economy, the first to hire coming out of a recession, and a likely place to start an enterprise of your own. But on the retail level that world was gone, and so was the neighborly service that came with the owner whose business thrived or sank on the goodwill of his customers.

I studied the map to see if there was a scenic parallel route. There wasn't. Not today . . . and for much of America not for tomorrow, either.

Day three.

"May I *help* you?"

I'd heard this before. Strolling with a knotty walking stick, crafted from a diamond willow as a welcoming gift by Connie's brother, I'd walk for a few miles every two or three hours on a country lane.

"No, I'm just stretching my legs," I'd reply to the friendly farmer driving by, concerned I might have car trouble.

But this was different. Returning round a bend, I saw a black pickup truck idling beside my car. As I neared I noticed the driver, a man in his forties with close cropped hair, was writing down my license plate number. A chunky woman sat next to him.

"May I *help* you?" he said, delivered more as an inquisition than a question.

"No," I said, pretending I didn't get his meaning. "But thanks for asking," I added facetiously.

"Alright," he said, and he eyed me once again before driving slowly off.

What the hell state am I in? Illinois. I thought the wackos were further . . . someplace else. I'd recently read that the United States now had more than twelve hundred home grown militias. I'd heard Canada had also begun to harbor a more virulent strain of discontent.Weird.

That night I pulled into a small town, and chose the friendliest sounding restaurant I could find, Sarah's Family Dining, just so I could reinforce my belief that these people were a tiny percentage of the population. Nevertheless, their feelings couldn't be easily dismissed. Beneath their suspicions, and often paranoia, was an anger at a world that wasn't working for them, a frustration that had to be taken out on something—an invasive government, a colluding world order, or whatever else inflammatory some kook had posted on the internet. None of which ameliorated how disturbing it felt to be held in suspicion in your own country for taking a pleasant stroll on a quiet country road.

Day four.

I'd been in most regions of the country, from New England and the deep South to luscious California, but for rustic beauty—pure sunny brook charm—southern Wisconsin outshined them all. Whereas Indiana and Illinois had fields as far as the eye could see, Wisconsin was rich in family farms. Rolling hills. Leafy trees shading black and white dairy cows. And every few miles an old fashioned red wooden barn.

It was a good place to spend the day. I'd woken with an admiration for truckers. How the hell did they do it? I'd only been driving for three days and I was whooped.

From here west the traffic should be more sparse, the driving easier. I drove down a breezy lane, past a few farms, feeling guilty that for them it was hard work, and for me it was a passing post card. The motel had told me about a park by a river, a place to pull out a book, spread out a picnic lunch . . . and vegetate.

That night I called Connie. "I think I've found it," I said.

"Found what?"

"My inner nothing. It's wonderful."

"I'll embrace it! What I need is a Caribbean island! Where are you now?"

"Almost half-way there."

"Picture a big smile!" she said.

Day five.

As I drove across Minnesota, my mind began to wander, as minds do sailing past monotonous terrain. Just what had I learned from my travels around the world? I had become half traveler and half tourist, not drifting from place to place with no set time, but not attached to my own culture either, able to compare, and then reject what I didn't like. When I fired myself it was the world that I wanted to see. And that's what I proceeded to do, cycles of six weeks home and a month abroad, from Europe to north Africa to the exotic Far East, more than thirty countries in all.

But how had it changed me? The answer, I hated to admit, was not very much. What I had expected was that the world would expand, grow more complex and mystifying, as I observed so many different peoples, each with their own history and cultures. And with that I would become more worldly and wise.

But instead the world seemed to shrink. For what I discovered was that we're all pretty much the same. Take away what we eat, to whom we pray, and a few other idiosyncrasies, and we all want the same things. We all want a good job, loving relationships, to feel productive, no suffering, and much happiness. Our needs and desires are really no different.

I stared out the window at a dust swirl kicked up by a green tractor. So after all that travel, I wondered, do I feel any wiser? No. But I feel more connected to my fellow man. I am more borderless and colorblind than I thought I already was, a feeling that I like when I turn on the news and see a foreign person.

As a result, I'm even more baffled when I read about ethnic conflict and military ventures, and think about how much global poverty and suffering the developed world still ignores. In the end, I guess, I want to tell young people, "Take the money you're about to spend on a Masters or Doctorate degree and travel. Shrink your world. It just might widen your sense of home."

Day six.

The Badlands. I like the sound of that. A fifty mile scenic loop, and beautiful it was. Incredible! Wind and erosion over time had left a jagged white landscape reminiscent of a science fiction movie and some kind of Armageddon. But the sign said there were bison. And that's what I wanted to see. It was amazing how the plains Indians had used every part of the animal: the hide for clothing, the skin to frame their teepees, the horns for glue, the ligaments for dental floss (or was that for bow string?). But the sign had lied. Not a one. Where do you hide a whole herd of bison? To think there was once a time when you could sit on a hill and a week would pass before the last of the herd rumbled by.

Interestingly, Banff has for decades hosted Indian Days. Someone felt it would be great for tourism to parade the Indians through the streets in feathers and full regalia. They could camp outside town for a spell and do dances and tell stories. Around that time bison were reintroduced and displayed in a paddock in view of the main highway.

"So let me get this straight," an observer might say. "First we shoot, maim and starve the Indians, forcing the survivors onto reservations. Then we do the same to the bison."

"Correct so far."

"Then we ask them to come back to help us attract more tourists."

"Correct again."

"Are we a forgiving nation or what?"

Just past South Dakota's Badlands, an hour or so, I came across the Black Hills National Forest. I knew this from the multiple billboards announcing Mount Rushmore. Who can pass that up? It has the faces of four Presidents embossed on the side of a mountain, an image every kid had seen a thousand times.

I turned off the interstate, and was surprised to see that an entire tourist town had been formed a few miles outside the monument. It seemed strange, like a whole town built to service the Mona Lisa.

I learned that the sculptor, Gutzon Borgium, spent years hanging off the rock to carve the granite faces. He was dedicated . . . he was obsessed. As American families, draped in Mount Rushmore extra-large T shirts, stared at the profiles in wonder, I could only think, "Was he nuts?"

Didn't anyone holler out, "What the hell are you doing up there, Gutzon?"

And what's more, the Parks Service, instead of leaving a simple wooded path to accentuate the experience, had constructed a mammoth stone entrance, an avenue of fifty flags, museum, amphitheatre, and gift shop (they forgot the ferris wheel), that almost overshadowed poor Gutzon's monument. Only in America, I thought, could we overdo what was already overdone.

It was late afternoon, the sun was beginning to set, casting long shadows over the hills, as I drove into Wyoming. I loved that name. And I loved the image on their license plates: the silhouette of a cowboy on a bucking bronco. The farms of the Midwest had turned into ranches, with horse corrals and names like The Big River ranch. As I experienced the country's transitions, from the hectic east to the industrial rust belt, to the corn husk farms, and now the wide open western ranches, I marveled at how much is missed flying to your destination.

Unfortunately, most of the small western towns had their store fronts boarded up. "Our biggest export is our kids," the bartender said. "There isn't much work around here," she lamented. I'd pulled off the road, calling it a day, and wandered into a bar for a beer. A cowboy, a man about my age, nodded in agreement. He was wearing a tan, straw cowboy hat and his jeans and boots were dusty. He appeared to be a little downhearted, though he didn't look like the type to complain.

"Do you work around here?" I asked, hoping to start a conversation.

"Yes. I run a ranch not too far from here."

"A big ranch?"

"I guess so, about five thousand acres."

"How's business?"

He took a sip from his beer. "It's been a long time since we had a good year."

"So what happens then?"

"We go into debt. I'm up to a half a million."

"Ouch."

"The seed's still got to be bought, and the equipment fixed. All I need though is one good year, and this could be it."

"Will that get you ahead?"

"No, but it'll get me even."

"And then it all starts again," I said, regretting my words.

He looked down into his beer. "Yup."

There was a moment of silence. "The choice," he said, "is having to give up the land; it's been in my family for years. I can't do that."

I suppose for some, if you have enough bad years, accumulate enough bad debt, you start selling off parcels so the banks don't take it all. I tried to imagine how he felt, trying to keep a family legacy, holding on with pride, while always digging yourself out of a hole.

Day eight.

"Where are you from?" I pictured someone asking me.

"Wyoming." What man doesn't want to say that. It beats the heck out of *Virginia* . . . what kinda sissy ass name is that!

"Where you headed?"

"Alberta."

"Alberta? What kinda sissy ass name is that?"

"It was named after Queen Victoria's princess daughter."

"Ain't that the place with the pink flower on the license plate?"

"It's not a pink flower. It's Alberta's Wild Rose."

"I remember now. Didn't they film that movie up there about those two gay cowboys, Humpback Mountain."

"It wasn't Humpback Mountain, it was *Brokeback Mountain*. And it wasn't cows they were herding, it was sheep."

"Sheep? What kinda cowboys you got up there?"

"Look, it was just a movie. A goddamn movie. They also filmed *Open Range* and *The Unforgiven* in Alberta. Where the hell are you from anyway?"

"Wyoming."

I headed up I-90 on my way to Montana. Just past the state line I pulled off the highway for gas. On the entrance ramp stood a woman hitchhiking. She had long black hair and she was holding a cone shaped drum.

"Where are you going?"

"Lethbridge. I'm hoping to get over the Canadian border tonight."

"I'm not going quite that far today. But I can take you as far as Great Falls."

She smiled and opened the door, and slid into the front seat, depositing her drum and a backpack in the back seat. Her eyes were dark and friendly and she had a ring pierced into her lower lip. But what I picked up instantly was that this was a genuinely happy person. There was also one other thing instantly clear. She was a full-blooded Indian.

"What takes you to Lethbridge?"

"I was visiting friends in Vegas. I'm on my way home to Edmonton. I'm out of money and thought I'd busk there a few days."

"Can you make any money at that?"

"Yeah sure, in the summer on a good afternoon you can pull in seventy or eighty dollars."

"Lethbridge isn't exactly a tourist town. Maybe you should try it in Banff, that's where I'm headed."

"I'll have to think about that. My family was from Morley, part of the Stoneys."

Morley was the name of the Indian reservation east of Banff between the Rockies and Calgary. There were three different tribes thrown together, which I'd heard sometimes resembled the Middle East. They were plains Indians, some of them remnants of Sitting Bull's Sioux who fled north after the battle of Big Horn.

"How did the Stoney Indians get their name?"

"I'm not sure. There's a couple of theories. They lived near the Rockies so they were called the stone people, which naturally morphed into Stoneys. Another theory was they used hot stones for their cooking. Maybe," she laughed, "they were just stoned all the time!"

"Do you live on a reserve?"

"No, I did for a while, but it wasn't for me."

I could see why. Most Indians seemed to do better integrating into white society. There were a lot of social problems on the reserves, from alcohol to drug issues. I'd also read some of the reserves were pretty corrupt. The chiefs, who sometimes ruled like petty tyrants, lived like kings while the people often lived in squalor. The government's guilt payments were a mixed blessing, helping on one hand while also contributing to unemployment. The Morley reserve had also been benefitting from their mineral rights, minerals that I'd heard were running out.

When revenue streams like these run dry, these same chiefs, in cahoots with the government and outside developers, have been known to foist casinos onto the reservations, in hopes of easy money. One can imagine what that does for the indigenous social problems.

"What's that?" I asked, pointing to a shimmering marsh land.

"That's a bird sanctuary. Birds migrate from the south, and I'm sure it contains . . . Listen to me. I am such a Canadian," she laughed, "pretending I know stuff that I don't know the foggiest thing about!"

We talked a bit more and then drove in silence for a while. This was big sky country. I looked in all directions. Huge puffy clouds hung above, so dramatic it seemed as though you could reach out and touch them. I noticed she had fallen asleep.

It was noon. I lightly touched her shoulder. "Let's get something to eat."

"How long have I been asleep?"

"About two hours."

"Wow, I must have been exhausted."

I'd stopped at a small oil slick in the road. The only place that was open was a small bar with a few pool tables. But it still served a mean bowl of pea soup. I picked up the tab and headed out the side door. She followed behind. The stairs were some kind of corrugated metal about four feet high. She looked down at her feet. "Imagine these shitfaced!"

A few hours later I passed a sign that said there were traces from the old wagon trains nearby. "Let's see that," I exclaimed.

"Cool," she said, and sure enough there were ruts in the sandstone near a creek from the covered wagons that once crossed the region. And not only that, there was a cliff face where the settlers had carved in their names. Names like, "Jenny and Randolf—1854." Some had written a little more, like, "William and two children—five months from home."

It was almost dark when we arrived in Great Falls. It had also begun to drizzle, and the weather had turned cold. "I'm pooped," I said. "This is as far as I go."

"Could you just drop me off at the highway? Hopefully I can get a ride. They won't let me hitchhike on the Interstate."

"Are you sure? It's miserable outside. Why don't you just stay the night. I'll get you a room. You can leave in the morning when it's sunny and clear."

"I'd still like to try. I'd really like to make it to Lethbridge."

I pulled over to the side of the road. There wasn't much traffic. She pulled out her knapsack and drum. Suddenly she didn't seem so sure. "What if I don't get a ride?"

"I tell you what. I'll come back. If you haven't gotten a ride you can stay the night here. How long do you want to try?"

"I'll try for an hour."

I drove away slowly. She stood in the mist near a sign with her hood pulled up and a piece of plastic protecting her drum. I drove into town and checked into a roadside motel. One hour passed. I drove to the spot where I'd left her. There was something disappointing about its emptiness. I guess I hoped she was still there. I sat in my car for a while, glad she was somewhere warm, and watched the rain come drizzling down.

Day nine.

I pulled up to the customs gate. He looked at me kind of sour. I think it's a prerequisite for the job.

"May I see your passport?"

"Of course."

"How long are you going to be in Canada?"

"I don't know, ten or twelve weeks."

He peered at me sullenly over his glasses. I knew I'd screwed up. Even though we can legally spend up to six months a year in each other's country they want to know *exactly* how long you're going to be there.

He stamped something on a yellow form, and said, "Drive your vehicle over to that shed."

I did, and out walked another customs official in a perfectly creased uniform. I swear even his tie was pressed. Next to him, after traveling for days, anyone would look like a criminal.

"Open your trunk."

I did as I was told, and he began rummaging through everything. I knew what he was searching for—a stethoscope, a hammer, anything that might indicate I was slipping up there to take a job away from a Canadian. I was too young to be retired, and he'd look at me in disbelief if I said, "You don't understand. I like being unemployed."

He reached the bottom of the trunk. "What's in those boxes?"

"Books. I'm an author."

"You don't plan to sell them up here, do you?"

"No. Unless you'd like to buy one."

Now how SMART was that?

He waved me through, and I hastened across the border, convinced he thought I was too mentally challenged to do any Canadians harm.

———·———

As I drove north I rolled past prairie towns. These small villages contained a half-dozen streets, a grocery stop with a gas pump, and a platform feed store. But what drew my attention were the grain elevators, wooden structures towering above twin railroad tracks. Many were freshly painted with the original signage still stenciled on the sides. Behind the elevators, undulating crops stretched into the horizon.

Connie had grown up on a dairy farm near a town called Leduc, an hour outside of Edmonton. "My father liked farming. He was a gregarious man, but he was tethered to the farm. Milking cows twice a day you couldn't travel anywhere."

Today Canada, western Canada in particular, is the world's largest exporter of canola, spring wheat, and oats. But that wasn't always the case. Connie's father had purchased one hundred and sixty acres, land like his grandfather's that was part of the Homestead Act decades earlier. Connie's ancestors were from Prussia, part of Germany then, and her father spoke German fluently. "Farming," she said, "was what he'd been taught. He was well read and loved history, but like most of these families he didn't have a formal education."

By the mid 1800s the end of the Napoleonic Wars had sunk Europe's economy, and the population stood on the precipice of starvation. Canada, at the same time, needed immigrants, hard working people willing to till its soil. And the government, followed by the railroad, sent a barrage of advertising to the weakened European countries. All of it was as sunny and hopeful as you could possibly imagine. "Free farms for the millions!" read one headline. "Homes for everybody. Rich virgin soil, land for mixed farming and cattle grazing," read another, above images of happy farmers and bonneted young ladies in fertile fields of wheat.

Canada offered one hundred and sixty acres of free land to any immigrant willing to cultivate it. The only covenant was that a quarter of it had to be cultivated within three years. A startling forty percent of the settlers failed. Out-migration matched immigration for a long, long time.

For what the bountiful and enticing ads neglected to show were conditions that the most hardened immigrants never expected. Settlers would sometimes arrive, barely off the steamship, only to find they lost their whole families in a matter of weeks to tuberculosis, cholera and malaria. Life on the prairie was desolate, and terribly lonely for people who were accustomed to villages and extended families. And all of this was magnified by the long winters. The cold could be fierce in the Rockies, but in the unsheltered prairies the cold seemed to just hang in the air, depressingly frigid beneath the shortened gray skies.

But if forty percent failed, sixty percent persevered, and like Connie's ancestors, who hoped life would be better for their offspring, they passed on productive farms to their children. Connie's father passed away ten years ago, and her brother continues to farm the land today . . . not far from Ukrainian domed churches, a reminder of a not too distant past.

I'd grown up in a nomadic existence, my father always viewing pastures greener somewhere else. In fact, I'd never lived more than two years in any one place before the age of twenty five. But there was something about Banff that felt like home. It was Emily Dickinson who said, "Give me the world's greatest city or the world's greatest wilderness, but nothing in between."

Maybe that was it. I'd had one, but was quickly finding out I relished much more the other.

In truth, I'd always be captivated by both, and maybe even needed both. In New York or Chicago I'd get off the train, stumble into the street, look up in awe at these manmade testaments to ambition, and think, "Damn, I've got to make something out of myself!" But in the Rockies I'd gaze up at the peaks ten thousand feet above, the sun coming down in shafts of light, and think, "God? Is that you up there?"

I turned north on Route 22, known as the Cowboy Trail, and the mountains came into view in the distance, still snow capped from the winter. And as I got closer to Banff I grew excited about seeing Connie, and my thoughts drifted to the B&B.

In the spring I had read about a B&B seminar being hosted at an inn in the Shenandoah Valley. Perfect, I thought, since I didn't even know what I didn't know. In addition to learning some practical tips I was curious about the people who would be attending.

There were eight couples thoughtfully assembled. Almost all were middle aged, and just like me they were anxious to separate being a guest at a B&B from the job of operating one. And from what the seminar host had just said I had a feeling only two would *happily* succeed. And the reason was that there were only two couples in which both partners were equally enthusiastic about creating and running a B&B.

The host felt it was worth elaborating upon. "This isn't an endeavor in which one partner can be merely supportive, no matter how well-meaning. It's often a full time job, it's a business in which your spouse suddenly becomes your business partner, and most importantly, it's a lifestyle. Strangers are going to be coming in and out of your life, under your roof, and you'd better both welcome that." A bit brusque, I thought, perhaps she saw a future as a customs officer, but judging from Connie's experience, it's better to be advised before HE or she is off playing golf while he or SHE is doing the breakfast dishes.

One couple had kids and asked how that would fit into the equation. I only half listened to her answer because I was thinking of Connie's two sons, who were teenagers when she launched the B&B. The oldest promptly moved into the garage while the youngest avoided the guests like the plague. "You can't really blame them," Connie said. "Most kids would soon tire of a stream of strange adults invading their space."

The couples' motivations were an interesting mix. A few viewed themselves as amateur chefs, trying out omelets and homemade truffles on their guests. A few were drawn to the remodeling, already picking out wall paper and period pieces. And a few were bored, and intrigued about a change in life.

Only two couples had chosen a property. One was a nineteenth-century stone farmhouse in the Pennsylvania countryside, and the other was an English cottage in Aldie, just outside of Virginia's famous horse country. I was just as new to the B&B business as they, but Connie had informed me of this. Like real estate it's *location, location, location.* Just because you build it doesn't mean they'll come; not if you're in the middle of nowhere, where you'll also need constant, costly marketing. Furthermore, if there's not much to do, the B&B will need to be the entertainment. That means hot tubs, swimming pools and whatever else you can imagine. And more critically, for your own sense of pacing, it means the guests will be at the B&B all day.

During the summer, the prime B&B season in Banff, nearly four million visitors come through the park's gates. And that's a lot of visitors! As a result, thanks to positive ratings on sites such as Trip Advisor and elsewhere, the B&B practically fills up on its own, with little to no marketing effort. "And though I'm proud of the B&B, it's not the B&B that the guests have come to see," Connie said. "They're coming to spend time in the mountains, to hike, raft, shop, explore and do a ton of other activities. For most it's a once in a lifetime trip. Each day, after a nice hot breakfast, they're gone. And then," Connie added, "I have a quiet house in which to clean the rooms, answer my emails, have a little time to myself, and get ready for any new arrivals that evening."

The seminar host closed with a nice thought. "Even though the reservations may have been made months ago, and to you it's now just a name in your reservation book, as they walk up your front steps, they envision you expecting them. So give them a nice friendly welcome. Then let them go to their room, use the bathroom and freshen up after a long day's travel, before telling them everything about your home they need to know."

One of the attendees raised her hand. "How do you know when it's time to get out of the business?"

"Where are you from? I'm glad you asked . . . Wyoming."

"That's easy. It's when you open the door and say, 'And what the hell do YOU want?'"

Reflecting back, I didn't seem to fit into any of the categories. I'd simply fallen for a lovely woman who came attached to a B&B. Would I enjoy it? I didn't know. I did like business, and I wanted to help Connie, and as I turned up Banff Avenue that was enough for me to try!

Chapter 6

. . . banned for life!

6:00 A.M. The alarm goes off.

"Up and at 'em!"

"I thought this was a bed and breakfast. I stay in bed while you cook breakfast."

"Very funny, American boy!"

"How many guests are there?"

"Just four. My mother will cook while you serve." Connie's mother had come down for a few weeks to help out until I got there. I'd had a full day's rest, though nine days in a small convertible and I'd rusted into a crunched position. I swung my feet out of bed, slowly. Nothing a shower won't cure.

Connie's mother was the ideal farmer's wife. She was dutiful, efficient, and didn't like to be around a lot of people. And that included me. The two couples were from Ireland and traveling together. They just checked in the previous evening for a three-day stay. Like most people on holiday they were in wonderful spirits. We chatted while Connie's mother handed me their plates.

Then I asked, "After breakfast would you like me to spread out the maps and circle several highlights to see?"

This was something I'd been practicing. It was a service guests wouldn't get at a hotel, and one they seemed to appreciate. Many of the travelers did a triangle, from Vancouver to Banff, and then north along the magnificent Ice Fields Parkway to Jasper. Some even added a cruise from Vancouver to Alaska. They had usually studied the guide books. But the guide books didn't cover some of the secret treasures only the locals knew, and more importantly the guests had no idea of distance. We could suggest itineraries customized to their age and fitness and interests, within their route and the time they had allotted.

I pulled out a local map first. "If you turn right out of our driveway and go straight for ten kilometers it will put you on the Minnewanka Loop. You'll pass Johnson Lake, Two Jack Lake, and circle around Minnewanka Lake. You'll probably see mountain sheep with huge curved horns licking minerals off the rocks. And there's plenty of elk. The mothers are calving now so give them plenty of distance."

"Are the bears out?"

"Absolutely." And I showed them where we kept the cans of bear spray.

"Aye jus ha ta run faster than you." One of them joked to his partner.

Then I told them to return by way of Tunnel Mountain, past Surprise Corner with a stunning view of the Banff Springs Hotel, and I circled the Vermillion lakes, the local hiking trails, and the three museums.

"Do we go through a tunnel?"

"Actually, no. The Canadian Pacific Railway had intended to run the tracks through the mountain, then found a more level spot further down, but they never changed the name. You probably heard the train whistle last night. It takes time to get used to it."

Then I spread out a day-trip map and highlighted Johnston and Marble Canyons, Lake Louise, Moraine Lake, Takkakah Falls, Emerald Lake and several other destinations. "At spiral tunnel," I told them, "you can see the front of the train coming out through one tunnel while the back end sneaks out another. It's an engineering feat. There's also an information center in town where you can get brochures on activities, and on your way back to Calgary you have time to take in Kananaskis highway. There's a visitors center there with a seven hundred-pound stuffed grizzly along with a stuffed cougar and wolf. You won't believe the size of the chest on the wolf."

Late afternoon Connie returned home from school. "How did you do?"

"Great, I think. Except for one thing. Your mother keeps giving me the stink eye."

"That's because she thinks you're a city boy."

"I am a city boy."

"So there you go."

"Very funny, Canadian girl!"

The evening cast a golden hue, and I gazed out the back window. The snow had only recently melted, leaving hundreds of twigs from the winter winds with patches of deer poop to be cleaned up. The deer would often sit in the yard for hours in the snow, peacefully safe from predators. But that was then and this was now, and with early buds sprouting, predators were the least of their worries. Connie would scream "Out!," at the sight of a deer while madly flapping a white trash bag.

Contemplating the yard work, my eyes settled again on the unpainted fence, and my thoughts drifted to Shane, the classic Western film about the laconic gunfighter who fell in love with the frontier woman. He was soon proudly, manly, mending her fences.

"Jamie?"

It was Connie. She had walked up behind me. Did she say "Shane?"

"My mother will be leaving right after breakfast tomorrow. Don't forget this when you're doing the rooms."

The sun slowly sets. The sky turns brilliant red. And just like in the movie the school marm retreats to the bedroom while the hero is left holding a toilet brush.

Connie's Banff Avenue B&B has three guest rooms. "It's the ideal size," she said, "beyond three or four rooms you can't run it yourself. You start needing full time staff. It becomes an inn."

From solely an economic perspective, even including Connie's busy summers, without a second income a B& B rarely generates enough income to support yourself, let alone a family. But it can certainly help pay a mortgage while living in a fabulous resort in a home that you couldn't otherwise afford. And for some, coupled with a pension, it could provide a transition to an early retirement.

But there's also another overlooked benefit. If over time you've built up the business with steady revenues, it's worth anywhere from three to seven times annual earnings added to the price of your home. Hence, $50,000.00 in yearly revenues can justify $250,000.00 added to the house price for a couple acquiring the home as a B&B.

Toilet brush in hand I surveyed Connie's immaculate B&B. Fortunately, like Connie, I am a neatnik. Some might hypothesize that a neatnik is someone with a perverse need to have physical objects neat and tidy, in order to create a life raft of order in what they see as a chaotic, unpredictable world. Then again we may just like the aesthetics of a pretty room.

Either way it's a convenient trait to have for maintaining a B&B. "Are the rooms clean?" is the most frequently asked question. (Slobs have it made. Left alone they create a mess. It's what they do. Then, burp, a neatnik comes along and cleans it all up!).

"Our home is your home," we tell arriving guests, and we mean it. We want them to feel at home. As you enter the front door, to the left is the living room with the stunning stone fireplace and picturesque views of the mountains. On the wall hangs a Robert Bateman print of two loons swimming in an emerald pool.

Straight ahead is the kitchen, a big kitchen, where we tell the guests they are welcome to store food and beverages in the refrigerator, "and help yourself to any of Connie's baked cookies and pastries." Open to the kitchen is the dining room with an oak table that comfortably seats six. It looks out onto flower boxes, and Connie's lovely garden.

To the left behind the dining room is our bedroom, separate from the rest of the house, that accommodates a bathroom and a small office space. Turning right at the front door are the three en suite guest rooms (a more melodious phrase in French parlance for *bathrooms in the rooms*), two guest rooms upstairs and one downstairs. Next to the downstairs guest room is a sitting room with a TV and shelves of books. Black and white photos of mountaineering at the turn of the last century, and an oil painting of a grizzly bear, adorn the walls.

The three guest rooms each gradually acquired a name; the Asian Room, the Hemingway Room, and the Grandma Room. Connie had spent a year in Japan, and she added Japanese fans and prints in the downstairs room as part of the décor. I added a silk painting from a trip to Burma. And that's about all it took. It doesn't take much oriental to dominate a room. You sort of have to go all or none. (It's like Chinese food. How many people have ordered egg foo yung and a cheeseburger or won ton soup and an Arby's roast beef, and lived to regret it? Way too many.)

The Hemingway room is my favorite. I named it myself, thinking Ernest Hemingway would have liked it. The mirrored dresser and night stand are dark rattan. A straw senorita sits atop the dresser. The window looks out onto Tunnel Mountain, and on the wall hangs an Indian peace pipe with five, count them, five tributes to wildlife; a deer antler, cow leather, horse hair, three eagle feathers, and tufts of coyote fur, amidst a red and blue beaded sheath. The Grandma Room looks just the way you'd imagine it.

I pulled out the vacuum cleaner. The B&B guest rooms had throw rugs on hardwood flooring. There was no wall-to-wall carpeting. "How come?" I'd asked.

"Carpeting creates smells. You can never get the odors out."

"Very smart!" I replied. "You don't teach third grade for nothing."

———·———

"Oh no! Now what do we do?"

It was Saturday, and Connie had decided she wanted a rock garden. This involved constructing a big mound of dirt, tucking in a black weed cloth, and then positioning a dozen or so colorful rocks in the dirt amidst gaily blossoming flowers.

Simple. Except for one thing. We didn't have the rocks. But we knew where to get them. This was the Rockies, for God's sake!

"The best place is along the river beds," Connie said.

So we drove my convertible out to the Minnewanka loop. It began to rain, but we weren't deterred. We found fascinating rocks, all shapes and sizes, and we stuffed them into the trunk. But we needed a big one, and I spotted it. It looked like a miniature mountain.

Half buried in the ground, we poked and prodded and finally levered it out of the soil, but it was too heavy to lift. So we rolled it to the car and with all our might hoisted it onto the passenger seat floor. A worthy task done!

But as we drove out of the loop, up ahead, Parks Canada had erected a road block. There were uniformed officials on either side of the road.

"Uh oh," Connie said.

"What do you mean, 'Uh oh?'"

"We can't take anything out of the park. It's against the law."

"We're not taking anything out of the park. Your house is *in* the park. We're just relocating it."

"Stop and turn around!"

"Are you nuts? They'll think we're terrorists! Put your jacket over the rock."

As we crept nearer it was obvious they were checking to see if drivers had purchased a park pass. I held mine up, smiled, and slowly drove by without stopping.

"That was close," I laughed. "We could have been sentenced to hard time."

"Maybe we'd get a reduced sentence," Connie said. "Since we'd be bringing our own rocks to break!" *

Narrow escapes aside, whoever coined the phrase, "Don't sweat the small stuff," never stepped foot in Canada! I'd already learned you couldn't swing a dead cat without hitting a bylaw regulation. Murder, drug dealing, and white collar crime may deserve leniency, but don't shovel snow off your sidewalk right away, stick a line with a worm on it in the lake without a license, or camp in the wrong spot, and the wrath of God in the way of a stiff fine will descend upon you!

Don't ask me. Ask Carla, a neighborhood teenager. She said she was banned for life, *for life,* from Safeway for stealing a Gummy Bear . . . .don't think Canadians didn't take heed!" **

———•———

Connie and I looked at the reservation book. There wasn't a day, from July through September, that we didn't have guests. "Perhaps," Connie said, "we should try to find some part-time help, two days a week, or we won't have any time for ourselves all summer."

"I think you're right," I said. "I'll put an ad in the paper, and, hopefully, I'll find someone you like."

"At least we're pretty light right now. There won't be any guests for the next five days. But then, while I'm at school, you're going to be on your own . . . and on your first day, there'll be six guests!"

"Six?" I replied, steadying myself for my dubious test as a short order cook. I pushed it out of my mind. In the meantime, I thought, relishing the task, I can learn a bit about Banff's early history.

---

*This little anecdote has caused Connie's Canadian mind much unrest and consternation. It is important to note, under the cover of darkness, her guilt overwhelming her, she placed the rock back in the exact same spot. She reminds all readers that rocks from the Rockies should never, ever be used in a rock garden.

**I asked a bylaw officer if he thought when little Carla was in her fifties or sixties Safeway might grant a reprieve?
   "Don't count on it," he replied. "We take our Gummy Bears seriously!"

Chapter 7
"Poof"

With some time on my hands, and a fascination with history, I went to the local library and poured through a dozen journals and books—hundreds, maybe thousands of pages—to understand Banff's early history. So here it is:

Twenty thousand years ago the Bow Valley was covered in ice. A shitload of it . . . two-and-a half miles high. Then ten thousand years ago it melted. Not overnight; like I said this was a shitload of ice. But it melted. Why? I don't know. Scientists back then wouldn't speculate without research funding.

Moving on. Out from under the ice came furry creatures. Lots of them. And rich Europeans loved fur coats, hats and gloves. So the Hudson Bay Company was formed, and in 1670 King Charles II of England, who apparently didn't give a damn about furry creatures, gave the company the rights to the fur trade, in all the land that drained into the Hudson Bay. I don't know how land drains either, but that's what Charlie said.

Well, hunting furry creatures is hard work. First you have to chase them. Then you have to skin them. So the company executives said, "Why not let the Indians do all the heavy lifting. We'll just trade them cheap crap for their furs."

The Indians eventually caught on . . . and the whole goddamn thing fell apart. The Hudson Bay Company wasn't making any money. Right about that time Canada became a country. 1867. But what good is a country without any land. Canada wanted the land rights back that had been given to the Hudson Bay Company. The company chairman looked at his balance sheet and said, "You can have it, and all the wascally wabbits that go with it!"

Finally, Canada was united. And what it dreamed of most of all was a railroad that would now join east to west. And it's here that Banff's history becomes more detailed, a captivating convergence of the Canadian Pacific Railway, a river, coal, and tourism.

A full decade before the Canadian Pacific Railway was incorporated in 1881, surveyors, not known for their sweet disposition, were hired to examine previous expeditions, and map out routes of their own for the best path to build the railroad through the Rockies. Most of their attention was focused on a northern route, since previous reports had wrongly indicated that the prairies to the south were too arid for agricultural production—produce that would be needed for transport to make the railroad profitable. In fact, a substantial amount of work had already begun in the north. No fewer than seven exhaustive surveys had been conducted.

But it was the advent of the Canadian Pacific Railway, where savvy businessmen demanded the shortest route, that much of the earlier survey work was overruled. For there was one geographic element that hadn't been considered enough, an element further south that may have already mapped out the route: the Bow River. Named for the bows that the Indians would craft from the saplings that grew along its banks, the Bow River started high in the Rocky Mountains at Bow Lake. Fed by glaciers and countless rivulets and rivers along its path, the river flowed eastward from the alpine ridges to the lower Bow Valley before winding its way along the foothills, past Calgary, and across the plains of southern Alberta. Finally, someone said, "Why don't we just lay the tracks alongside the river?" (I think it was the great grandfather of the guy who put the wheels on suitcases.)

Whole books have been written about the river—its turquoise beauty from the glacial silt; the varying sediments along its bottom; its use for hydraulic power, sports and recreation; and how it impacts the alpine ecosystem. But here's what I remember most. Drowning was the second leading cause of accidental deaths in Alberta, and the Bow River contributed to the statistics. (The first was heart attack when you hit the freezing water . . . actually, it was being crushed by heavy mining and agricultural equipment.) The river was dangerous to cross. Currents swept away cattle, horses and people. Crossing the ice was unpredictable. There were fissures in the coldest times, and in the Spring, temperatures melted the ice from the bottom up, making its thickness hard to detect. A safety valve, long forgotten, was the use of a pole. People would traverse the ice with a long pole horizontally under their arms.

But what was critical to the formation of Banff was the sensible decision to build the railroad along the path of the river, a waterway that could also float logs from the timber camps since sixteen hundred railroad ties were needed for just a half a mile of track.

And it was along the river, past the alpine heights as it wound its way on the valley floor that a surveyor for the Canadian Pacific Railway stuck a marker that simply read, "Banff Siding # 29." That's all Banff was, a railroad siding named for Banffshire, Scotland, the birth place of the C.P.R. President. And that might have been all it was for a long, long time except for one other thing. Trains run on energy, and that energy came in the form of coal. The Bow Valley, it was rumored, had an abundance of it. And that, and that alone, would be enough justification for laying the tracks in Banff along the Bow River.

Coal is formed from vegetation that grew in swampy areas millions of years ago. The waste accumulates, creating a thick layer of rotten matter. Over time, tons of mud and sand build up over this layer and slowly compress into rock, mainly shale and sandstone. Subject to ever increasing heat and pressure this rotted matter hardens into coal beds. And the Rockies contained all the essential ingredients—time, heat, and pressure—to facilitate huge coal deposits.

Seams were found behind Cascade Mountain, where Bankhead, a mining town just minutes from Banff, was erected. Bankhead was populated by Eastern Europeans: Poles, Romanians and Ukrainians to name a few. And behind a slag heap was a Chinese camp, made up from workers left over from the railroad, who were said to keep to themselves, tending their small gardens, entertaining themselves in the evenings by gambling.

But any rosier views were more than offset by the dreary work, all day in dark, cramped spaces where methane gas and flooding were a constant threat. Nevertheless, it was coal that the C.P.R. needed, and until the 1920s it was just outside Banff that a noisy, pounding, smoking tipple separated the coal from a conveyor belt, and day after day provided it.

The railroad was finally completed, the last spike driven in on November 7, 1885. With a directive to not exceed a two and a half percent grade, I shudder at the immensity of the project. I can imagine a conversation with one of the Chinese laborers shanghaied to construct it.

"Here, this is for you."
"Wassat?"
"Dynamite."
"Wah I do?"
"Light it."
"Wah I do then?"
"Wun. Wun like hell!"

It was also during this time that the North West Mounted Police had been sent in to keep the peace, which euphemistically meant protecting the C.P.R. while the Indians, who had been pushed onto reserves, looked upon the building of the railroad through their sacred hunting grounds with a resounding, "What the fuck?"

With their ceremonial red tunics, brown hats and riding boots (there are still a few who pose for pictures each summer in Banff) the Mounties inspired stories of Sergeant Preston of the Yukon, dog sleds, bon mots such as "the Mountie always gets his man," and most importantly, the sale of thousands of miniature red Mountie dolls peering out of Banff's tourist windows.

But now that it was built, the railroad needed money. The Canadian government even placated the railroad's investors by giving the C.P.R. thousands of acres alongside its tracks that the railroad could sell to settlers, providing the agricultural products it had banked on to transport produce to the rest of Canada.

But that wasn't enough. The railroad needed people, rich people, and thousands of them, to ride the rails westward and make the railroad profitable. What they needed, and they didn't even know it, was tourism. And they got it. They got it in droves when, serendipitously, three of their employees on leave stumbled on an underground pool of water, hot water, stinking like rotten eggs, that would soon be hailed for its medicinal qualities. It was a tourist-generating engine that would outmatch the World's Fair. Banff's newly discovered hot springs.

Rain and glacial melt had dripped into the limestone of the mountain, and seeped deep underground. It then rose to the surface full of minerals, warmed from the earth and smelling like sulphur. The government, seeing its tourist potential, ended all claims by the three men, and designated the area Banff Hot Springs Reserve.

None of this was lost on Dr. Robert Brett, whom I envision to be a roly-poly sort of man. Brett was originally brought to Banff as the medical practitioner for the railroad. Whether he was a quack or a genuine healer, only he knows. But if anything, he was enterprising.

Perhaps even a cousin to many modern day doctors and dentists who see an M.D. degree as a license to gouge the public. (Easy there, fella. This is no place to discuss the elephant in the room impacting Canadian and American soaring health care costs.)

Dr. Brett was well aware that natural hot springs were believed by many to have healing powers. Maybe *yes*, maybe *no*, he must have thought, and he soon opened the Brett Sanitorium at the head of Banff Avenue, known for its restorative powers, where he piped the hot spring water six hundred feet to his crippled and arthritic guests. As an added treat he bottled the water and sold it as "Lithia Water," a "cure for what ails ya."

But even Brett's business creativity was diminished in size by William Van Horne's, the General Manager of the C.P.R. An earthy bon vivant with a taste for fine porcelain, Van Horne recognized that tourism was essential to the success of the railroad. "Since we can't export the scenery we'll just have to import the tourists," he said.

With an amateur's passion for architecture—he loved to doodle and sketch imposing structures—and a circus promoter's knack for illustrations and words, "May I tempt you to leave England for the vast forests and stupendous peaks . . . ," Van Horne was anxious to begin luring passengers. And what he envisioned was a network of luxury hotels along the train's westward route, luxurious enough to entice the crème de la crème.

But none of these resorts would equal the grandiose vision he had for the Banff Springs Hotel, built atop a site with stunning views of the mountains, only minutes from the now famous hot springs. Looming above the trees, overlooking the Bow River, the hotel was modeled after a French chateau. The interior was finished in native pine and fir. The lobby was a magnificent glass-domed octagonal rotunda. There were reading rooms, parlors, billiard and smoking rooms, not to mention a large bath house with mineral water from the sulphur hot springs. But probably most popular of all was the ballroom. This was the gilded age. And the hotel guests could be seen arriving with trunks full of clothes, including tuxedos and evening gowns for the orchestra led dances.

But Van Horne realized that even the rich needed more than mineral baths, afternoon teas, and dances to fill their idle time. They needed snowshoeing, horse riding, mountain climbing, and whatever other pursuit he could imagine to entice them. And luckily for Van Horne it wasn't long before hungry entrepreneurs with names like Brewster, White, Peyto, and Luxton—names still known in Banff today—began filling the nooks and crannies of the local tourism industry, from pack horse excursions and outfitters to mountain guides, and publishers. If there was a vacuum to fill they filled it.

So there you have it. Thanks to the C.P.R.'s advertising of a majestic wonderland, and a pool of magical water, Banff at the turn of the last century was a bubbly cauldron of dukes and ladies from the carriage set, atwitter with chefs and hoteliers, merchants and opportunists, with a fair share of rounders, riff raff, and squinty eyed Swiss guides.

But what strikes me as fascinating is from mining and timber to transport and tourism, from hotels and restaurants to real estate and construction, it's hard to imagine a company with a more mundane name, the Canadian Pacific Railway, that operated as a more powerful conglomerate.

Its tentacles and influence would have rivaled the notorious Hudson Bay Company. And though Banff is a critical hub of a nationally designated park, it was also, for many years, very much a company town.

Chapter 8
"Sweet"

"What do you do besides this?" Norman asked.

"Nothing really." I cracked two more eggs and began stirring.

"Nothing?" he repeated. He was a kind looking man, a retired student counselor, a career spent looking after others.

I turned the hashed brown potatoes. "You know what they said about the British aristocracy. They did nothing. And they did it very well!"

"By the way," another guest asked. "How far is it to Lake Louise?"

"About forty minutes," I replied, as I opened the oven door and checked the English muffins. Oh no, they're starting to burn!

"Do you have any more coffee?"

"Coming up," I said, and I finally got everything cooked and all six guests served. This ain't easy, I decided, cooking and serving a full table while juggling a slew of questions. A tilt-a-whirl would be less dizzying. Pretending is half the battle. They seemed to think I knew what I was doing!

After breakfast I went over the maps. Norman was in his mid-seventies. He was moving slowly. His wife, though, was full of energy and anxious to get started. She'd laid out a busy agenda.

I cleared the table, put everything away, and checked-out one of the couples, helping them carry their suitcases. Then I began cleaning the rooms. I noticed on Norman's nightstand there were several bottles of pills. It was noon when I stepped out onto the back deck with a sandwich, and realized I had been going non-stop for six hours. Feeling nourished, after lunch I spent a few hours raking the leaves and twigs. It felt good to see the yard begin to take shape.

It was late afternoon when Norman and his wife returned. "How was your day?" I asked.

Norman's wife exclaimed, "It was wonderful. We hiked Johnston Canyon, and even had time for Lake Louise. Her husband smiled, and I watched as he cautiously made his way up the stairs.

A couple checked into the B&B a few minutes later, and, shortly after, Connie walked in the front door.

"Did you ask them if they had any allergies, or if there was anything that they didn't eat?"

"Oops, I forgot," I said, and I pictured a hapless guest prostate on the floor, his eyes rolled back in his head. "I'll ask when they come down for breakfast."

It is here that I might note that my sweet and demure Connie had turned a bit crabby lately. "Crabby?" said one of her colleague's husbands. "My wife passed crabby two weeks ago. She's now a functioning psychopath!"

Teaching was Connie's calling. As a child she practiced on her younger brother and sister. Connie's first two years were spent teaching grades one through six in a one-room schoolhouse. And many a late night in bed she'd be grading her students' work, or engrossed in the next day's lessons.

But as she limped toward the end of the school year her nerves were frazzled. "I'm done. The kids are done. I'm just babysitting now."

And it's here that I jumped into the lion's den. There was a little girl named Fatima that I encountered on a journey to Turkey's coast the previous year. She was eight years old, the same age as Connie's students. She was selling souvenirs. I bought a purple scarf she'd made with sea shells sewn onto the edges, and a small metal box and bracelet. I also took a photo of Fatima sitting in front of her stone home. I told Connie that I brought the stuff with me, thinking she might like to show the kids.

"They'd love it," she said. "But why don't you present it to them yourself?"

The next afternoon I ambled three blocks to the elementary school. Some classes were outside on recess. I glanced at the jungle gym. Those aren't children, they're monkeys!

Connie's class would be different. I arrived early, thinking I'd sit in the back for a while and watch Connie teach. I walked into the classroom and suddenly twenty-two eyeballs swiveled in my direction. Now what?

"Mr. MacVicar is going to talk to the class about his trip to Turkey."

A little girl smiled. She was missing her front two teeth. "How much did the tooth fairy give you?" I laughed.

"Twenty-five cents!"

A boy piped up. "I get fifty cents." Another joined in, and in seconds the whole class was chattering. They were out of control!

Connie didn't yell or scream. She lowered her voice almost to a whisper and said in the flattest monotone you ever heard, "Please take your seats." It was masterful. I looked for a seat myself.

The class gathered at my feet, and amidst raised hands and questions, and fidgety, unstable limbs, I told them about my trip. As I stood to leave they became more frenetic. They were volunteering for something, anything, "Can I fold the scarf?"

Meanwhile, a little girl kept tugging on my sleeve. She was persistent. Annoying. "Yes?" I finally said.

She looked up with a bucky beaver smile, "I read at a sixth-grade level!"

"And I bet your penmanship is perfect too," I said.

She nodded affirmatively, and in that moment I wondered if I'd gone back to the future. Could I be taking in a pig tailed Hillary Clinton?

I gotta get out of here! I grabbed the scarf and box and exited toward the door. A little boy, out of nowhere, hollered, "Bite me!"

I think he was talking to Hillary. Twenty minutes and I was exhausted. Connie, I decided, can be as crabby at the end of the school year as she likes!

———·———

That night I noticed Norman sitting by himself in the TV room. He'd apparently had another full day. "Good evening," I said. "Mind if I join you?"

"Not at all," he said, and I noticed how thin his voice sounded.

"You've been doing a lot," I said.

"I'm afraid a bit too much. I just had an operation a few months ago, and my wife thinks I need to be out there doing things. But I'm just not up to it."

"She seems determined," I said.

"Yes, and I'm not sure what to tell her."

I had the feeling that their marriage had lasted forty years by his figuring out what she wanted, and just doing it. "This is your health Norman, and you need to listen to your heart . . . maybe you can say, 'I know you mean well, but I just can't do what I used to. Feel free to do things on your own, but I need to rest. I need to go at a slower pace.'"

They went out to dinner, and I hoped I hadn't overstepped my bounds. Connie too had begun to worry about his health.

The next morning, after breakfast, Norman sat alone, and lingered over his tea longer than usual. "What do you plan to do today?" I asked.

"Nothing," he smiled. Last night I talked to my wife. We're going to do nothing today. And we're going to do it very well."

———•———

There were three replies during the week to my advertisement for summer help. The first was a chef, a nervous man who had trouble making eye contact.

"No way," Connie said. "He'd drive me crazy! I'd be shopping for exotic mushrooms to keep him happy."

The second looked like Jesus, with a surf board and an Australian accent. "What's your story?" I asked.

"Just here for the summer, mate, you know?"

Actually I didn't, but I launched into a thorough description of the job just the same, after which he stunningly replied, "Sweet."

The third was a charm. She was nineteen, her name was Briana, and she was from Moncton, New Brunswick. "I'm in Banff until mid-September, and then I go back to college. I'm majoring in tourism," she said. "I've got a night job, but I could use more income. I promised my father I'd be saving for school."

"Can you cook?"

"I sure can."

She was perfect, personable and enthusiastic, and she also spoke fluent French.

Canada is a bilingual country, which means the French are expected to speak English, and the English are expected to speak . . . well, er, English. One of my personal goals was to learn another language. So I immersed myself in French, since the French went everywhere that I loved to vacation. After night courses, audio tapes, and hundreds of hours of self-study, all I can say is, "I am a window."

That night Briana returned and met Connie. "You're hired!" Connie said. "Come by this Saturday at 7AM and I'll give you your training. You can start next week. We'll do Tuesdays and Wednesdays."

Chapter 9
The Hermit of Inglismaldie

Connie and I heard that there was a new bed and breakfast opening in town where an old cabin once stood. "They're going after the upscale market," Connie said. "I hear they're going to be charging three hundred dollars a night."

"Let's go see it," I said.

We walked past Elk Street and Caribou Street and into the back streets of Banff, where the tourists rarely go. The streets are all named for wildlife; we live on the corner of Banff Avenue and Beaver Street, where someone has notched chew marks on the wooden sign post.

It was early evening and Connie and I loved walking through the neighborhood. There's something about meandering past homes—unruffled homes on quiet streets—that gives the impression all is perfect in the world, including the lives of those inside. It makes for idle talk that brings Connie and my worlds together. "What would you think of a greenhouse like that in your yard? A red door, that's kind of nice. What do you think of the scalloped tiles on that roof? Those would look great on the B&B."

The nice thing about Banff is no two homes are alike. History and the personalities that went with it unfold as you walk by, from someone who lovingly built a Swiss chalet, to a log cabin, to a modern alpine house with cedar siding. Every house is different. Some, like the Bankhead homes, have historic markers in front.

You can tell if it's a Bankhead house by looking at the windows. For some architectural reason the upstairs and downstairs windows don't align. They're diagonally off by a noticeable margin.

There are still five or six large Bankhead houses in Banff. Bankhead was the mining town ten miles north of Banff that was run by the Canadian Pacific Railway. Labor conditions led to a series of strikes in the early 1900s. At the same time the coal seams were thinning. The mine had been reduced to manufacturing brickettes used as cheap fuel for cast iron stoves. But the provincial government took a share of the mining revenues and when another strike broke out in the early 1920s, and the CPR refused to negotiate, the government ordered the CPR to settle the strike or move their three hundred dwellings off the government's land. And that's exactly what the CPR did. They demolished the industrial buildings, but moved the church and all the homes, one-by-one on flat bed trucks, to scattered locations across the province. From the school house and the boarding house to the multitude of homes, all of the cement foundations are still there, with aspen trees growing out of their cellars. And that's all that remains.

Connie and I strolled down to the river where the houses seemed to compete with one another for size. With no regard for his neighbor's view, a garish mansion was being built with imposing eaves and balconies. Wouldn't a penis extension be cheaper, I wondered? (I know what you're thinking. You're thinking about Donald Trump again. Now stop it. That's rude!)

We finally arrived at the new B&B. "It's going to be nice," Connie said. "They're even putting in an underground garage."

There are three types of B&Bs in Banff: those that cater to the wealthy (and there are two in town that do that well), those that serve backpackers with shared rooms and kitchen facilities, and those like Connie's that are priced for the mid-level market.

B&Bs in the U.S. started as cheaper alternatives to hotels, but over the years that's been reversed. In Canada, B&Bs are still thought of as the more economical option. Regardless, Connie and I share the same view: that our guests should leave feeling as though they received far more than they paid for. But I suppose Connie's pricing reflects our tastes; we like serving people like us, guests with more moderate dispositions, and priorities similar to our own.

———

"Come on," Connie said. "Briana's all done, and the rooms are finished. Let's go out to Johnson Lake. There's something I want to show you that only the locals know."

We drove out to the Minnewanka loop and parked in a gravel spot by the lake. There was only one other car there. It was a two-mile hike around the lake with the eastern side exposed to the sun. We passed a path closed off by environmentalists protecting an inlet where loons were known to nest. Then we climbed to a high ridge where the water shimmered below, and the whole valley stretched out before us.

On the other side the trail wound its way along the water's edge through pine and fir trees, past buffalo berry bushes that would ripen with red berries in August, just in time for the bears to fatten-up for the winter.

"It's back here," Connie said, and she turned into the woods by a fallen tree.

"Where are we going?"

"To the hermit's cabin," Connie answered, and sure enough, in a clearing surrounded by trees, sat a dilapidated log cabin with a rusted tin roof. There were remnants of an old stove along with some pots and pans on the ground nearby.

I ducked my head, and stepped inside. "Look, you can see a dark shadow where an ice axe and a frying pan once hung on the wall."

"There's a sign over there that tells the story," Connie said.

How strangely and wonderfully Canadian, I thought. There was a laminated sign by a tree twenty yards from the cabin, but nothing on the trail that indicated the cabin even existed.

Originally from England, Billy Carver, according to the posting, built the cabin in 1910. He lived by himself for twenty-seven years, working in the mines periodically, but mainly hunting, fishing and trapping, and somehow living off the land.

I stumbled on a book about two young men during the depression who took one look at the soup lines and said, "We can live better than this," and moved to the back woods to do the same. For them, tracking had a more serious purpose, and it was along the animal paths that they set their traps. There was nothing glamorous about trapping that has been mythologized in movies and coon cap lore. Animals were known to chew their foot off to escape the steel teeth, and the government took pains to outlaw the wire garrotes hung above ground that slowly strangled the animal to death.

But it didn't appear as though Billy Carver had any commercial interests. A sympathetic store keeper sometimes brought him flour and supplies, but otherwise he was seldom seen. In 1937 two local boys discovered Billy in pretty bad shape. The local police took him to a nursing home where he later passed away. The police said that there was no legal reason they could find for his seclusion. From what I gathered, he was simply a misplaced soul who sadly couldn't connect with the human race.

———•———

I opened my email. There was a message from my publisher, a small press that specialized in quality books on the entertainment industry. I couldn't believe it! Was I reading it correctly? *The Advance Man,* a seventeen-year project, had been named a finalist for The Marfield Prize: National Award for Arts Writing.

My head was spinning. This was the only national award devoted exclusively to non-fiction books about the arts. A previous winner had been knighted for the achievement by Queen Elizabeth. There were few national literary awards in the United States. To be named a finalist in one of them meant the book shared the honor with one-tenth of one percent of all published books that year.

How sweet the vindication! The larger publishers wanted cost cuts that would have impacted the quality, and I'd refused. One thing that I had learned after a career in the arts is that fame, money and recognition are ephemeral; what's permanent is pride in the work.

And in the end I'd beaten nearly all of them. Press releases had been sent out by the awards committee to all the media. And then I waited . . . nothing. Nada. Not a single publication that I'm aware of, including *Publisher's Weekly*, published the announcement.

I wandered up to the Hemingway room. A voice reached out, "Tough luck, kid."

And here's the thing. Sadly, I had company. *The Washington Post* published the finalists for the PEN/Faulkner fiction award, and didn't announce the names of the books. The Pulitzer Prize for non-fiction was announced on the PBS "News Hour," where the viewers were told if they wanted to see the interview they would need to go online.

Woody Allen said, "I don't want to live on through my work. I want to live on through my condo." While still here, though, I'm confident he enjoys being recognized for it.

None of this is the case in Canada. Literature and language are revered in Canadian culture. There are several literary awards and the honorees are celebrated in the media. Publishers, partly for sustainability but largely because of their value to society, are subsidized by the government, as are many of the other arts.

"You want recognition, kid, you need to be an actor," the voice stepped in. "You get feted for pretending to be someone you're not, and you get twenty takes to pull it off. I couldn't stand Spencer Tracy, the guy who played the old man in the sea. What a miserable bastard, you should have seen the way he treated Katherine Hepburn."

This isn't helping. I'm making myself feel worse. Where was I? Oh, yes. It's been said there is no other medium in breadth and depth that can match the terrain of a book; not a song, a play, a film or a documentary. Consequently, books are more than an art form. They're part of our human development . . . and American media would rather cover a movie star's latest break-up.

But it's not just literature, it's also language, and Canadians hold it in higher regard. I'm sure there are examples proving me wrong, but thus far I've yet to meet a Canadian, regardless of education or class, that didn't speak with clear enunciation and diction. Culturally, in these two disciplines, Canada, long ago, left America in the dust.

"Whachutalkinbout?"

Chapter 10
"Smokin!"

One good thing about starting off with six people is from that point forward serving four is a dream and two is a piece of cake. I'd slowly fallen into a pattern, and with Briana helping two days a week, I could focus on other tasks.

The fence still looked daunting, days of scraping and staining both sides. So I fixated on the barbeque pit. It was a heap of scraps that hadn't been used in years. Connie's sons were in town; they rented a truck and heavily dismantled the cinder block walls surrounding the grill.

I carried the sticks and twigs from the barbeque pit to a spot across the street that was overgrown with weeds. Combined with the twigs and branches that I'd already been collecting, the stack of brush was beginning to grow high, very high. Bylaws isn't going to like this.

But then the pile began to shrink. No sooner did I add to the stack then the next day it disappeared. Who was my helper?

I finally spied him wobbling back to his cabin. What saved me was the town drunk. Come rain or shine, every night he cooked outside while entertaining his friends with bottles of wine. No quicker than I added to the stack did he stagger over and take an armful back.

We had become symbiotic, no different than the bird who sits on the back of the hippo eating the bugs the hippo can't reach.

———•———

"I scare. I scare."

Two pretty girls from Taiwan had arrived at the B&B; Emmy and Judy, they had given themselves American names.

I spread out the maps. "Perhaps you'd like to go up in the gondola. It takes you to the top of Sulphur Mountain."

Emmy put her fingers over her mouth and giggled, "Nooooo . . . I scare. I scare."

"Then you might think about horseback riding. Warner's stables is on the other side of the bridge."

Emmy covered her mouth again. "Nooooo . . . I scare. I scare."

Judy looked on, smiling sweetly. I didn't have the heart to bring out the bear spray.

"I tell you what. I've got a few hours," I said. "Why don't I give you a tour." And I drove them around the Minnewanka loop.

———•———

Connie and I joined some of her friends and went out for an evening of entertainment. It was a Canadian trio belting out funny songs. And then the spokesman made a joke about Americans, a comment that poked fun at Americans' arrogance. I expected a chuckle or two, some muffled laughter, but it practically brought down the house. A stranger in a strange land, I suddenly, profoundly, realized there was a pungent strain of anti-Americanism among Canadians. As an American with Canadian roots, I was taken aback.

Unfortunately, Americans have grown to feel a sense of entitlement to the riches of the world, (though this isn't a new phenomenon, we stole the name America after all; even France didn't name itself Europe) and over time we've conveyed that attitude in subtle and not so subtle ways—a sort of "We're Americans, aren't you delighted we are here?" demeanor that sometimes comes with the luggage. I've noticed this on rare occasions at the B&B. While the person is conversing with other guests at the breakfast table, an empty coffee cup reaches out toward you, or you get up in the morning to find an empty pizza box discarded on the kitchen sink. It doesn't happen very often, but when it does, it's too provoking to be forgotten.

But, of course, it's complicated. Canadians respect Americans for much of the same reasons others do: America's entrepreneurial spirit, its inventiveness, and its unmistakable drive. And from what I've observed Canadians are intimidated, to the point of sovereign over protectiveness, by America's size and influence. Economically, Canada has always needed America far more than the reverse, though that perception may be changing, for Canada is rich in resources increasingly in demand by China and other developing economies.

But I think what really offends Canadians, and may be at the heart of the anti-Americanism that Canadians are far too discreet to show, is America's indifference. The opposite of love is not hate, it's indifference, and Canadians feel Americans are simply indifferent toward them. Rick Mercer, a comedy TV show host, demonstrated this using Canada's popular cafe donut chain, Tim Horton's, as bait. He went with a camera crew to Princeton University, and began interviewing professors and students.

"What do you think of our Prime Minister, Tim Horton?" he asked a student.

"I think he's fine, I guess," the student replied.

"Do you think Canada should continue its seal hunt in Toronto?" Mercer asked a professor.

"Well, not if it's bad for the seals," the professor responded.*

---

*An American diplomat volunteered this: "Would it help if I told Canada that outside our borders Americans are clueless about ... everything?"

———•———

"Honey, I have to go to Costco. Will you come?"

Costco, just the thought of it made me ill. I'd rather poke myself in the eye with a sharp stick. Costco was a huge discount warehouse in Calgary where Connie bought her food and supplies for the B&B in bulk. How could I say no?

"No."

"Come on, please, we'll have fun."

"Okay, but don't say I'm not doing my part for international affairs. And I'm bringing my calculator."

I used to tell students, don't worry about the money. Just do what you love and the money will come. But I never believed it. Until I met Connie. She has absolutely no interest in business. I asked if she had a chart comparing by month each year's revenue to another. Her eyes glazed over. So I made up a chart. Then I asked, "What are your food costs per person per meal?" No idea. So I'm bringing a calculator. It's how I intend to survive Costco.

Connie laughed, "I told you, I just sort of backed into the whole thing."

"Why fiddle dee, Miss Scarlett, I don't know nothin' 'bout birthin' no babies!"

"Why Rhett, ah knew you'd understand."

And it's here that I might explain why Connie and I get along so well. We never fight. Annoy one another, yes. But we never fight. Because we have rules. We've made a pact. For example, we can't say, "Whatever" in the middle of a spat, which we both know means, "You are such a moron."

Nor can we say, "Fine, fine . . . fine," which also means, "What a moron!" Plus all things negatively directed such as, "How many times do I have to tell you to take your shoes off in the house?" must end in "darling." (You don't want to play footsies with a Canadian. Next to the Japanese they have the world's cleanest floors, and the world's dirtiest feet. Disgusting . . . darling.)

We've even been debating about allowing an acronym, WYPJST— pronounced just the way it sounds—interjected into the conversation when needed in public. It means—you guessed it, how many times have you whispered it yourself?—"Would you please just shut the fuck up!"

But we see the world in the same way. Our interests are often identical. And we converse easily, about everything. As you grow wiser and more mature, you realize it's these things, like water flowing together, that bonds the relationship.

But those are all practical matters. What really works for me is I think she's HOT. Just this morning I said, "You're smokin!"

I knew she liked it, because she smiled when she said, "Whatever."

"Ten dollars."

"Ten dollars what?"

"That's how much breakfast costs for each person. I figured you secretly wanted to know. So I told you."

"Keep thinkin', Butch," Connie laughed. "That's what you do best!"

Chapter 11
If You Don't Like the Weather . . .

The weather looked overcast today. The French couple at the table pouted just a bit, shrugging their shoulders in resignation. I said that I'd heard it was different at Lake Louise, nice and sunny, and they cheered up, "Voila!"

"Voila!" I said in return. I love the French. I spent time in my travels with a French family. Imagine the world without France. How drab it would be! And the French women . . . no wonder the English invaded so much! But—and this cracks me up—their stories always have a *but* in them, something to make you feel woeful.

"I was at the boulangerie today, and met your friend Anna."

"Oui. Oui! Anna, I love Anna. I always buy my baguettes at her bakery. She has the best bread in town!'

"Yes, I really liked her. What a pleasant woman."

"Always smiling."

"Indeed."

"But . . . "

"But what?"

"But, you know, her husband left her last year."

"He did?"

"Yes, it was horrible. She was a wreck. The children were a mess. The whole village was sad, it is traumatic."

"I see," I say, suddenly feeling miserable for the happy Anna I had just met. So I switch subjects.

"Your neighbor Pierre came by this morning. He brought you fresh carrots and lettuce from his garden."

"Pierre! What a sweet old man. He loves to work in his garden. The entire town loves him. But . . . "

"But what?"

"He broke his hip last year."

"He did?"

"Yes, it was awful, in two places. He fell on his hoe. His poor wife found him. Everybody felt terrible."

"*Tres triste,*" I reply, shaking my head, now feeling terrible, too, for poor Anna and Pierre, and wishing I had never met them.

So making the French couple happy this morning made my day!

When a guest asks, "What's the weather going to be like today?" I usually quip with a smile, "One thing about the Rockies is if you don't like the weather, just wait ten minutes," adding, "We get all four seasons here. We just get them in the same day!"

And this is the thing, I'm telling the truth. The Rockies has a weather system all its own. Impossible to predict. It isn't unusual to leave a bright and sunny Calgary, only to arrive ninety minutes later at the entrance to the mountains in a blanket of ominous clouds, and vice versa. And the weather inside the Rockies, often only minutes up the road, can be just as dramatically different.

Banff sits at an elevation of 4,000 feet. And many of the mountain passes are a thousand feet or more higher. The peaks and valleys trap clouds and moisture in the air, and the bright snow caps reflect the sun's heat back into the atmosphere. Airplanes often experience turbulence flying above from updrafts and downdrafts. And what any of these five things have to do with one another I have absolutely no idea!*

But I know that the weather can change in an instant, which is dangerous for hikers who set off comfortably in shorts and t-shirts to find themselves shivering uncontrollably later in the day. Hypothermia can easily take root, causing dizziness, confusion, and unhappy endings. People think hypothermia results from freezing temperatures. Not true. It comes from sudden temperature changes of twenty degrees or more, and that can happen during any season. Getting wet or wading through shallow, freezing streams can quickly lower your body's resistance.

Yet the Rockies are predominantly sunny, offering a toasty warmth most days of the summer. It's a deceiving tropical sun, and I've learned to apply plenty of sunscreen. It's a desert-like climate. And it's dry, very dry. In the winter tiny creases on your fingers from flossing string quickly crack into irksome cuts that take forever to heal. Moisture creams only last a few minutes; the dryness comes from within. You have to daily consume three times the amount of water that you'd normally drink. We keep a jug of spring water for the guests to fill their bottles before venturing out for the day.

Every year we get Chinooks, wonderful baths of balmy air in the middle of the winter that warm the valley for two or three days at a time. You can see a Chinook coming by the clouds, where a strange-looking horizontal funnel sweeps across the sky. At the start, though,

---

*Norman Sanson, whose 1867 signature graces one of the stones in the B&B's fireplace, erected a weather station on the top of Sulphur Mountain, and climbed the two-hour trek to the summit every week to take meteorological readings. He furthered our understanding of the Rockies' strange weather patterns.

Andrew Ackerman, from the Department of Environmental Sciences, sourcing *The Handbook of the Canadian Rockies*, offers this explanation: "Influenced by the proximity of the Pacific Ocean, weather can change rapidly as eastward moving air currents from the Pacific cool as they are forced rapidly up west facing slopes, then just as quickly, drop over the crest of the Rockies, onto the flat plains."

fierce winds from the Chinook come out of nowhere; gale force gusts that shake the trees. Hiking in the woods, it's a good time to crawl under a log; the shallow rooted pines can topple like twigs, leaving the landscape resembling crossed pick-up sticks.

Understandably, visitors who have traveled thousands of miles are disappointed when it isn't a perfect, sunny day, but there is beauty to the moody days, when clouds and mist are passing among the peaks. It's hard to gaze up at the craggy cliffs and not imagine mountaineers up there in the dark clouds, and I always feel relieved that I'm not one of them.

The Canadian Rockies do experience all four seasons, but the spring and fall are short. The trees are not as diverse as elsewhere, but the Aspen trees turn brilliant yellow, and there are red and auburn bushes to accent the foothills. The winters are long, but so are the summers. And when I hear of cities suffocating under sweltering, humid conditions, we are hiking in spring-type temperatures for days on end, among wild flowers that seem to sprout everywhere. These are also days that are uniquely longer, for during the summer it remains light outside well into the night, playing havoc, I suspect, on parents trying to coax their children to bed.

———•———

I'd never worked side-by-side with a woman I loved in an un-stressful task. It was a new experience . . . and it was nice. The B&B was work, but it wasn't stressful. We awoke with a shared idea, to try to shape the contours of the front yard. Patches of green grass wound around Connie's new rock garden, highlighting landscaped areas of flowers and small stones while providing a quiet spot for a curved stone bench.

But what the yard needed was mulch—rich, brown chips of wood and bark to encircle the trees, and separate the elements with a natural path. We donned old jeans and sweatshirts, and after raking the last of the winter debris, we drove to the garden shop. Mounds of mulch awaited us. While Connie held the bags I shoveled them full. The bags filled the trunk and back seat, and together we worked all day in the yard.

Late in the day I sat on the front stoop, and Connie came and sat down beside me. Paired in dust we looked out at what we'd accomplished. We didn't say a word. There was nothing that wasn't already being said. Her arm came around and rested contentedly on my shoulder.

———•———

It's Sunday morning," I said. "We've got nothing we have to do. Let's head up to the Columbia Icefields Parkway."

Our destination was the visitor's center, about a three-hour drive, two-thirds of the way to Jasper, where the Athabasca glacier sweeps out of the mountains, so close to the highway that you can drive to the base of the glacier, and walk out onto the ice.

Just past Lake Louise we turned right onto the parkway. The route narrows to a bumpy, two-lane road. We passed Bow Lake, where a log-built lodge sits in view of Bow glacier, the eponymous source of the Bow river. On our left we passed Peyto Lake, splendidly outfitted in glittering turquoise.

But what's spectacular about the drive is the mountains. One minute you're looking out at magnificent peaks framing the distance, and the next moment you are driving right alongside them with avalanche warnings telling you not to stop. The rock faces take on a more colorful hue, from grey to yellow to, at times, a speckled burnt orange. Waterfalls, hundreds of feet up, cascade out of the crevices from the melting snow and ice that's accumulated all winter on the crests, and deep inside the mountains.

Many who have spent time in the American Rockies comment that the Canadian Rockies are more dramatic, more vertical, and can be experienced at a closer range. No doubt the harsher Canadian weather has chiseled the rock faces to a sharper, more jagged surface, with walls of rock that often ascend straight up for thousands of feet.

But the fundamental difference is the rock itself. The Canadian Rockies are composed of sedimentary rock—mainly gritstone, sandstone and shale. The American Rockies were a combination of sediment and granite, in which over time the sediment has eroded away exposing the granite. But the formation of the mountains was similar.

About 200 million years ago the North American continent began drifting northwestward. At the same time a much harder, denser shelf under the Pacific Ocean began to move northeastward. And it's the impact of the collision that created the Rockies.

As the Pacific floor pushed west to east into the softer sedimentary layer, it pushed the sediment upwards, like the folds of a rug being pressed forward from one end. And here's what's fascinating: though the formations occurred over a period of 125 million years, the wrinkly folds from the upward pressure are still strikingly visible. The sight would bring any devout creationist joy, for the wavy folds make it appear as though the mountains were created in a day, like the molding of a simple piece of pottery.

Through erosion the Rockies look very different then they did sixty million years ago. For one thing, in the beginning they rose to heights of 18,000 feet above sea level, almost twice as high as most of the peaks today. But more importantly, glaciers that began 25,000 years ago and ended 14,000 years ago, recent in geological years, sculpted the mountain faces and valleys that we see today. It was the last of the glacial ice advances that began 1.8 million years ago.

Connie and I drove north, rounding a huge curve in the road where boulders the size of small houses had tumbled into the valley below. We climbed to the top and behind us stretched one of the most beautiful views I had ever seen. Two mountains divided by a roaring river crossed one another in a majestic sweep, like two crescent moons linked together.

We continued on, and slowly the glaciers began to appear on the crests of the mountains, the first of eight major glaciers fed by the Columbia Icefields. They went on for miles, hundreds of feet thick, formed by layer upon layer of snow, as much as twenty feet per year, compressed into ice. One of the glaciers had a hole carved out, concaved and the color of robin egg blue.

But the glaciers had begun to shrink. And when we arrived at the visitors center there were photographs of the Athabasca glacier as it appeared a century before. It had lost half its mass and receded almost a mile, leaving a moraine of broken rocks in its path. The good news is that over the eons, glaciers have ebbed and flowed, advanced, and then receded. The bad news is that this time, man may have had a hand in it.

Scientists still haven't connected humans as the cause to much of the recent volatile weather, from excessive floods to increased tornados, but they are in general agreement about the source of global warming, with human emitted gases trapping heat in the atmosphere with the warmer air soaking up the moisture.

The problem for the Canadian Rockies is that those same furry creatures that King Charles wanted to eviscerate still take winter shelter under the snow, both to hibernate and as protection from predators. Snow is cold on the surface, but warm and insulating down below. Whole ecosystems of sub-species and plants that thrive in the snow would be put at risk with as little as a four-degree change in climate. Not to mention the fact that it's the snow and glacial run off that feed the rivers and streams that flow to the parched prairies where water is vital for agriculture. We couldn't build enough dams in the world to store the amount of water contained for free in the winter snow pack.

There is also a multiplier effect. Sunlight reflects off the snow and the glaciers, and the less there is of each the more the heat is simply absorbed, thereby raising the temperatures, thereby shrinking more snow and glaciers. Suffice it to say we have a problem, but is the trend reversible? As H.R. Haldeman, of Watergate notoriety, said, "Once the toothpaste is out of the tube it's hell getting it back in."

Connie and I drove down to a parking lot not far from the base of the glacier. We had to walk along a winding trail, and then up a steep path strewn with rocks and ruts, and then stroll down the other side. It wasn't as easy as it looked.

The wind was blowing off the glacier. It was freezing. The air was thin, gaspingly thin. And the dusty path was straight up.

"Connie," I whined.

"What?" she replied, looking back, the key word being "back."

"I can no longer see out of my left eye!"

She ignored me. So I concentrated on the sway of her hips. Serves her right.

We finally reached the top of the hill and began our descent to the foot of the glacier. But as we approached the huge, hulking white mass, warning signs, one after another, began to appear. "Venture out onto the glacier at your own risk! It can result in instant death."

I looked up and noticed several visitors hiking in a roped off area on the glacier. Another sign appeared, posted on the side of the trail. This one told of the death of a young man who fell into a snow covered crevasse not fifty yards from the base, and died. A third sign noted that rescues must take place within a matter of minutes, which is almost impossible. The reason for your quick demise is that you're likely cut and bleeding from the razor sharp edges during the fall, glacial water is running under the surface that you are now half dangling in, and you are wedged in tighter than a knife in a block of Swiss cheese. I'm surprised the last sign didn't suggest that you save everyone the useless trouble and just blow your brains out!

Connie and I arrived at the bottom of the glacier. We touched it with our toes for good luck, and decided that was far enough.

It was late in the afternoon and we began our drive back to Banff. We had only driven a few miles when we noticed a van and two cars stopped on the side of the road.

"I'll bet it's a bear." Connie said. "It's the perfect time of the day."

We rolled up slowly to the head of the line and pulled over. Sure enough there was a young black bear eating dandelions just a few yards from the road. "Dandelions are a delicacy for the bears this time of year," Connie said.

I heard the door to the van behind us slide open. A French man, speaking to his friends, got out. He was holding a camera. His wife and another couple looked on. The bear scurried off beyond some trees. The man followed, disappearing himself, behind some bushes.

His wife, I believe, should have an interesting story. "It was a lovely day. Jean Luc had never been happier."

"But . . . "

Chapter 12
"The Bears Are Out."

If you suddenly come across a grizzly or a black bear, which is always a possibility since they use the same trails we do, and the bear begins to act threatening, here's what you need to know. Does the bear just want me out of its territory *now*, or does it want to eat me?

This presupposes that you are not standing between a bear and her cubs, for if that's the case, the inside of a crevasse will feel like a day at the beach. But here's why you need to know. How you react, and how you defend yourself, depends on the bear's motives.

Here's what I have been told. Most animals are territorial, so whether the bear is immediately threatening or not, stop in your tracks, take out the bear spray, and slowly start backing away while talking in a human voice (versus what, an armadillo's?) so the bear will know that you are not prey. Do not run, or the bear will quit dithering, and conclude that you are fun...and prey.

If the bear is being territorial or defensive it will act agitated, pawing the ground, snorting, sniffing the air, and behaving angrily. And it may charge. It may be a bluff charge. Either way, now's a good time to use the bear spray. Incidentally, while considering your options, bears are agile swimmers, they can easily climb trees, and they can run as fast as a horse.

If you don't have bear spray, or it's not effective in stopping the bear, promptly lie on the ground face down, and clasp your hands behind your head for protection. One swat can easily remove your scalp. If the bear thinks you are dead it may be satisfied that you are no longer a threat, and leave the area.

If instead of behaving agitated the bear is acting sneakily, walking slowly toward you, eyeing you shiftily, or you observe that it's been stalking you, then it likely sees you as lunch. Use the bear spray, and fight back with everything you can!

But all this can happen in a matter of seconds, hence you may not immediately know the bear's intent. So this is what a hiking brochure advises. I'm not making this up. "Lie on the ground and be still. If the bear is still chewing on you after five minutes it's not being defensive. Begin fighting back!"

I can see Connie hollering down from a tree, "You're doing great honey! Only three more minutes to go! Would you like that in one-minute, or thirty-second increments?"

This is why I'm more scared of a black bear than a grizzly. A grizzly is probably acting defensively, and making noise while hiking can help deter a surprise encounter; whereas, black bears have been known to stalk you to eat you. A black bear, which can top three hundred pounds, is half the size of a grizzly, but their strength and jaw pressure are enormous. Picture even a small one, and think of a two hundred pound pit bull with claws. What they do is knock you down, taking away any advantage (which is none) that you might have had.

A grown man was recently bicycling down the Hoodoo trail, possibly blocking his sensory perceptions while listening on headphones to music, when a one hundred and eighty pound black bear charged out of the woods, bounced him off his bike, and dragged him fifty yards into the forest. His screams of help were heard by two other bikers who raced into town for help. He was rescued, but not before incurring serious injuries, including an arm nearly severed from his shoulder.

So despite their cuddly features, bear encounters can be dangerous. But would the Rockies and the wilderness experience be anywhere near the same without them? (It is important to note that incidents like this are very rare, only happen to locals, and never, never, never happen to tourists who bring money to spend. For more information contact the Alberta Prosthetics Association.)

But this is the bears' territory that we have imposed ourselves upon, and though they're not yet on the endangered list, there are those who rightly are doing everything they can to maintain their population. Unfortunately, the development of golf courses and houses continues to encroach on their territory, making encounters more likely, encounters in which the wildlife eventually loses.* But another chief culprit, an enterprise that has cost the lives of countless bears over the years, is the railroad.

The highways have been cordoned off by fences, but the trains travel right though the wilderness park. Grain seeps from the train cars onto the tracks, and the bears naturally feed on the spilled grain. And for some reason the bears don't move. In addition to sealing the cars better, which hasn't solved the spillage thus far, there have been numerous creative suggestions. One idea submitted is a contraption that would roll ahead of the trains and emit a harmless, but effective, taser-type shock to any wildlife on the tracks.

---

*A wildlife officer told of killing a three-year-old bear he'd come to know well, a bear that had become habituated. "This is part of my job, a part that I despise." Summoned to a subdivision where the bear repeatedly went for food, the officer recalled, "the smell of gunpowder mixed with the sweet, sickening smell of blood. As the bear gasped his last breath I only wish that all those people who contributed to this could have been there to share this moment with us."

The protests against the CPR on this issue have become noisier lately, so in response the railroad has just designated one million dollars to research the problem. This has been going on for two decades! What don't they know? Wouldn't the money, I wonder, be better spent on the solution.

Connie and I continued our drive back to Banff along the Icefields Parkway, and spied two more black bears in a meadow. "The bears are out," Connie said, an annual revelry previously announced in the local paper, heralding the arrival of spring.

I came around a corner, and suddenly we saw a large black bear crossing the road ahead of us. I slowed to a crawl, and watched it almost disappear in the woods, walking north through the forest, parallel to the highway. I quickly turned the car around.

"Where are you going?"

"I spotted an old logging road a ways back," I said. "We're going to pull into the trees and wait."

I crept ten yards into the narrow dirt road, and stopped, and then turned off the car engine.

"We're just going to wait here?" Connie asked.

"Yup. The bear was headed in this direction. It should cross this road in a few minutes."

A photo recently appeared in the paper of a grizzly walking along the Bow River, right by the town gazebo. The zoom lens made it appear as though it was only a few feet from the photographer, and likely the last picture he ever snapped. The bear, though, just kept walking, swam across the river, and retreated to a clearing behind the horse corral where elk had been known to graze. Parks had been keeping the elk and their newborn calves out of the townsite in order to keep the bears at a distance. Only a few weeks prior a family had awakened to a blood curdling scream. A grizzly had attacked an elk calf in their back yard.

The rangers had tagged a few of the bears known to frequent the nearby area. One in particular was called Bear 71. She had been sighted near Banff for years, and never acted aggressively toward people. The only encounter in which anyone got hurt was a young man who saw the grizzly one night on the way up Tunnel Mountain, and ran back so fast he landed in the hospital with multiple scratches and bruises. The rangers had been keeping a close eye on Bear 71, not because she posed a danger, but because she had given birth over the winter to two cubs. Just the other day she was spotted near Vermillion Lakes with her two cubs playfully in tow.

A female grizzly will be in heat each June for about three weeks. The male, crossing her range and lustily aware of this calendar, will shadow her constantly, grooming and nibbling her ear until she stops playing hard to get, whereupon they will mate repeatedly for days, at times up to an hour a romp. A biologist grinned, and said, "Who's going to tell them to stop?"

Impressing the female for sex is serious business. The male often battles other males, and is left with scars, broken teeth, gouged eyes and concussions. Bears are no different, and they don't even have helmets and shin guards to wear for protection!

When exactly does a bear enter its winter den? Cold and snow obviously have something to do with it, but the timing depends on having enough fat reserves, especially if the bear is pregnant. During the fall a bear will increase its weight by as much as forty percent in preparation for hibernation, mostly from berries, pine nuts, roots, and ants, which are high in protein.

Like most animals that den for the winter bears do so to conserve energy while food is scarce. They hibernate up to six months, with their heartbeat dropping from fifty to only ten beats a minute. But they're not asleep. Hike off trail, and accidentally step on a den, and the bear can become very alert.

Interestingly, bears are the only mammal that give birth during hibernation, right in the middle of winter, almost always toward the end of January. And it's then that the potbellied balls of trouble begin nursing from their still hibernating mother. Typically grizzly cubs will nurse up to two years, every two or three hours, though they'll begin eating grasses at four months.

There are three times as many black bears as grizzlies, and grizzlies have fewer cubs. Though wolf packs have been known to hunt them, bears have few natural predators, except one: other bears. And larger bears have been known to attack denning bears and their cubs. All the more reason the news of Bear 71 and her cubs was treated by the town with keen interest.

"Look!" Connie said. "There it is."

"Patience," I teased, "is a virtue."

Not more than ten feet in front of the car the bear had emerged from the forest. It stopped and stared at us, not moving, as curious as we were. Grizzlies and black bears can be similar in color, so I looked for the tell-tale hump that a grizzly carries on its shoulders. There was none. This was clearly a full grown black bear, and with glistening hair, a healthy one at that. We gazed at the bear for several minutes, until finally the bear disappeared back into the woods.

"You know what amazes me?" Connie said. "The silence. They walk through the woods and you don't hear a thing."

Chapter 13

Sad

I opened a celebratory bottle of wine! Connie's school year was finally over. She had come home with a bag of goodies, chocolates and small gifts from her students' parents, with lovely notes of thanks. As she opened the tributes one-by-one, no longer were the kids the little cretins of only yesterday, but sparkling squishy tykes to be replaced by a new batch next year. And so begins the teacher's cycle once again.

"You must be exhausted," I exclaimed. "Why don't you visit your sister for four or five days, and take a well deserved break?"

"How nice of you," she said. "But right now it's such a relief to have just one job, running the B&B, that I'd rather wait. Let's see how we hold up over the summer."

———•———

I strolled down to the post office, past the high school fronting busy Banff Avenue. Their school year still had a few more days to go, and there must have been two hundred kids milling around the playing field.

I stopped for a minute, frozen by a picture that I'd rarely seen in recent years. There was not one boy or girl, not one, that was overweight. Every single teenager was fit and trim.

It made sense in a way. This was a small town, and all the kids either walked, biked, or skateboarded everywhere. But just as relevant, their parents were outdoor enthusiasts, skiing, hiking, snow shoeing, and taking advantage of every activity a beautiful alpine setting has to offer.

I looked out at the kids, comparing them, I suppose, to others elsewhere, and a slice of dialogue from David Lean's *Lawrence of Arabia* came to mind. Peter O'Toole is reclined on his elbow in the sand, under the twilight sky, when his Arab guide inquires excitedly, "Lawrence, tell me about your country! What is it like?"

"It's a fat country," Lawrence replies. "The people are fat."

"But you are not fat Lawrence."

"I know," he says. "I am different."

———•———

I walked into the office of a well recommended dentist in Banff. A small piece of filling had fallen out.

"It's just two small holes, easy to patch," he said.

"Great," I replied. "Let's do them now."

Canada has what's considered to be socialized medicine, cradle to grave government-provided health care. And it's often been cited in comparison to the U.S. But as one Canadian put forth, "If you think your health care is expensive now, wait until it's free!"

From what I've observed Canadians pay about twenty percent more in taxes than U.S. citizens, plus Connie still pays an insurance premium of $150.00 per month to overlay what isn't covered. So for the average citizen the comparison isn't cost, it's the quality of care. And in Canada, particularly the big cities, the waiting time for almost anything can be dangerously long, occasionally forcing those that can afford it to fly to the U.S. for time-sensitive operations. On the same token, millions of Americans have for years had no health insurance at all. Many can't afford it. If they are diagnosed with cancer, and don't have the funds for treatment, they are simply sent home to die.

In terms of the ever spiraling costs, like any capitalist system, the only effective solution is supply and demand, good old fashioned competition. Personally, I'd flood the gates with certified doctors and dentists (on both sides of the border reports have indicated that the profession has often limited the number of practitioners), post their fees online, and let market forces do the work, cleansing the market of those that are over-charging. If increasing the supply of doctors meant subsidizing their education many would be fine with that, if it meant we didn't have to subsidize their billings. One pediatrician I know of bills out $4,000 a day just on office visits. How do you explain that to a struggling mother of two?

But herein lies a dilemma, a catch 22 when it comes to controlling costs. If people don't have insurance or government coverage, we have a catastrophe. Few can afford the more complicated health care necessities. But as long as the *insured* patient is only liable for a fraction of the costs he doesn't complain about the charges to the doctor, which eliminates the start of healthy competition.

I exited the dentist's office. The patient preceding me had a $700 bill. She was told her share was only $68. The rest was charged to her Canadian insurance. She paid the bill and walked out without even looking at the $700 in charges.

I was handed a bill for $260. I have no dental insurance coverage. It was for ten minutes worth of work, two tiny patches that didn't even require numbing. I asked to speak to the dentist. "This is outrageous. You only did ten minutes worth of work. Have you lost sight of what people have to do to earn $260?"

"No one else complains."

Lawrence would have been proud, "I know . . . I am different."

He reduced the price by half.

———•———

I picked up the local paper, and casually turned to page three. A headline read, "Grizzly bear killed on the tracks near Bow Valley Parkway."

I read on. It was the same old story. The bear had been eating grain on the tracks. The bear, the article went on to say, sadly, was a bear well known to the area. She had recently had two cubs. It was Bear 71.

A camera had been mounted on the front of the train. It captured a tragic image. As the train bore down, the mother grizzly reared up, and charged the locomotive in an attempt to protect her cubs.

The cubs were only thirteen months old. If the rangers took them in and began to feed them, the cubs would never survive again in the wild. All the rangers could do was keep an eye on them, and hope their mother had had enough time to teach them to forage on their own.

The news story offered a hopeful sign, the cubs were last seen sticking close together. Attracted by the perfume smells, they were spotted in a meadow where their mother used to take them, feeding on wild flowers and dandelions.

Chapter 14
Geese and Stores and Wily Politicians

Animals take votes on matters that affect the group, at least geese do. I was meandering around Cascade Ponds when I noticed a flock of Canada geese sitting peacefully past the bridge. There must have been fifty of them. I stood and watched these beautiful birds for a moment, and what I had once read came to life. A few geese began honking, and then a few more, and pretty soon the whole flock was a cacophony of sound, and then they all flew off. Geese will honk in agreement or disagreement as to whether they should stay in their present spot or move on. It takes a sixty percent majority for the group to agree to get the show on the road.

Imagine if we made them more human. Then they'd need a constitution, a supreme court, congress, parliament, and four hundred legislators, and the geese would never fucking go anywhere!

———•———

It was time to start on the wooden fence. Now that Connie was home I'd have some time in the afternoons to move forward. I wandered down to the hardware store on Bear Street and picked up a wire brush, a scraper, and three gallons of paint, mixed to the color of a redwood stain. It was a small store, part of a chain, well lit, and tidy. It was orderly, almost too orderly.

I had stumbled on a description of a general store in the 1930s that had served the area for years. It was fascinating, for it conjured up a sweet nostalgia for a time when things weren't quite as tidy. The town, you see, was in an uproar. "I've never seen the locals so upset," Connie said. And what made the folks so riled was equally absorbing. It was a tale about *change*, in which the geese, the store, and what was about to happen all had something in common; change doesn't always come easy. But first, a general store nearby in an earlier time as described in a book, *Canmore, The Story of an Era*:

Appearing like a soaring wing, one mountain in particular graces the town of Banff like no other. Mirrored in the Vermillion lakes, Mount Rundle, standing 9,838 feet high, was named after a missionary, Reverend Robert Rundle, sent by the Hudson Bay Company in 1840 to live among the Stoney Indians.

And it was after Mount Rundle that the Rundle Trading Store was named. "The store was painted dark yellow, and had a wooden platform running along the front. The building was close to the railroad tracks, which was convenient for loading new merchandise into the basement.

Inside the store were four departments: groceries, hardware, butcher shop, and dry goods. The grocery department handled almost everything. Canned goods were piled high on shelves reaching to the ceiling. In front of the shelves ran a long counter, the front of which was made of glass compartments, showing samples of cereals, raisins, and nuts. At the back of the counter were drawers and bins from which clerks ladled out other commodities. Candy jars ornamented the counter, and children would wait for the bigger hand of Ernie Colebrook to scoop out their nickel's worth.

The butcher shop was a marvelous place, with sawdust on the floor, a huge chopping block, and quarters of beef to be unhitched from a hook in the ice house, placed on the block, and cut just to please you. Presiding in this department was the affable butcher, Charles Skates. Liver sold for ten cents a pound, a fresh crab was a luxury at twenty-five cents, and a pig's head, for head cheese, came cheap, sometimes with an eye still in it.

Thursday was fish day, because that's the day an assortment of fresh fish, surrounded with ice arrived from the coast. Butter from the Cochrane dairy could be bought in twenty pound slabs. The hardware department had everything hanging or piled up; including dishes, tubs, ladles, chain saws, jerries, and the most popular pick and axe handles.

The other half of the store was partitioned into a boot and shoe department and dry goods area. Piled on the counters or shelved to the ceiling were boots, rubbers, mine shoes, moccasins, skates, 'Stanfield' underwear, needles and pins, bolts of yard goods, ladies' dresses, and every kind of mine clothes. Then to please the elite, men's measured suits could be ordered. Twice a year a salesman brought in large packing cases of women's dresses and coats. The back of the store was used for storage and furniture, all of it, sound, and practical. And it could all be put on your Rundle Store account." But that was then, and this is now.

"I teach and I hike."

"I write and I hike."

"And we both run a B&B."

This was our mantra. Over and over we'd repeat it, for Connie and I knew if we became embroiled in local politics and the latest incendiary issue we'd cease to enjoy the tranquil beauty all around us. But this was too juicy to ignore. The town had been pushed over the brink.

For years, a small bookstore, the Banff Book and Art Den, had nestled itself quietly near the river on Banff Avenue. It was a cozy store with wooden trim, run by a couple that had done exceedingly well catering its literary tastes to the community. But the couple had recently announced the store was closing its doors. Indigo, a major bookstore chain, was opening a branch in Banff, and that was the last straw. What with Amazon, ebooks, and now this, there was no way they could compete. The townsfolk were up in arms. This was emblematic of one more local store being replaced by a bland and faceless chain. Didn't Banff already have enough chain stores, let alone a plethora of touristy trinket shops?

Friends of the couple circulated a petition. No more chains. And soon they procured four hundred signatures. It didn't matter that the couple had made up their mind, regardless; the locals were fed up with seeing the character of the town slowly disintegrate. The petition was handed to the mayor and the city council. From a steady drumbeat, to a gathering storm, to an outright roar, the citizens of Banff demanded a hearing. Op ed pieces sent in by the residents denouncing the arrival of Indigo and criticizing the town council began to appear in the papers. (Allow me to digress for a moment about op ed pieces. In Washington you could bluster in a letter to the editor all you want, and unless you are Henry Kissinger, the *Washington Post* is never going to publish it. This is a small town. There are two weekly papers. They need news. You send it. They print it! The sender will then run into whoever they just lambasted . . . everywhere.)

Anyhow, this could no longer be ignored. The citizens were too restless. The mayor announced a special meeting, a public forum in which everyone could air their grievances.

Finally, Canadians were acting more like Americans. A good old fashioned donnybrook was in the making. I couldn't wait. No longer would we Americans stand alone with a report card reading, "doesn't play well with others." This was war!

Well, not quite.

Connie and I arrived at the high school gymnasium where I expected to see a head table seating the mayor and town council in front of a hostile audience, microphone in hand, ready to pounce.

Instead four hundred chairs faced . . . well, each other. And the mayor and city council sat among us. They had hired what they called "facilitators," who, standing in front of large easels, would take down our concerns. "This is the input we need," said the mayor. And we then broke into orderly groups.

After it was all done all I could think was, *they did it again.* Canada's report card would rhapsodize, "goes along, gets along," with five gold stars on top.

As we filed out I noticed the facilitators tearing off the sheets with our colorful scribbling, and placing them in a stack. "Do you think the council will study all this?" I asked Connie.

"Are you kidding," Connie replied, "of course not. This was about quelling the natives, letting us vent, the council can't tell the landlords who they can rent to."

Connie was right. What they could control, which was the exteriors that blended into the town architecture with rundle rock and cedar, was outstanding. But he who owns the property can rent to whom he pleases. And the problem, and the source of the misdirected anger, wasn't that the town council didn't want unique, locally owned stores; it was that the rents were too high for the independent proprietors to survive. Five locally owned stores had folded in the last year alone. I'd even heard that landlords were levying what they called a "key fee," a charge of up to fifty thousand dollars to existing tenants just to renew their lease; this after years of slowly building their business. The chains could operate at a loss if they chose, just for the international exposure a tourist town brings, but the small local owner could not. Nevertheless, the demise of the small bookstore had tapped into a frustration and a question that had been building for years. How in the face of today's competition could citizens preserve the small town sentimental feel they had hoped would never leave?

I couldn't help thinking that what I'd just witnessed locally also played out on a national stage. Most Canadians, and allow me to put this delicately, don't think their leaders give two hoots about what they think, which isn't much different from how most Americans feel. But the difference is that Americans think they can do something about it. Why? Because all the way up to the President, Americans vote for nearly all of their representatives, and if those elected ignore the more vocal protests, voters harbor the thought, and rightly so, that they can vote them out of office.

Canada, like Great Britain, has a parliamentary system of government, based on an aristocratic view that the voters should elect the members of parliament at the local level, the "riding" in Canada. And then it's "Thanks, we'll take care of it from here, off you go now. Bye, bye," and the majority party then decides who to anoint as Prime Minister, and who should run the country. Of course, the aristocrats would argue, and sometimes correctly, that in America if there are enough imbeciles in a given state, don't be surprised if you end up with an imbecile as Governor. And don't be surprised if strategists on a national level use "swing states" in a tight national race to elect a half-wit President.

So is one system better than the other? I suppose it depends on who you ask: the geese, the store keepers, or the wily politicians.

————·————

"Hey sweetie, what do you think?" I stood back, and admired my work, a six-foot section of fence, freshly scraped and painted.

"It looks great! Only two hundred feet to go!"

No problem, I thought. I dipped my brush. "I write. I paint. And I help run a B&B."

Chapter 15
"Beep beep"

Connie was preparing the fruit plates while I set the table for breakfast when two of our guests strode in, a German couple, athletic, and used to alpine hiking. "How was your day?" Connie smiled.

"Fantastic!" the man replied. "We saw a pack of wolves."

"You're kidding," I exclaimed, thinking they'd probably seen coyotes. Two packs of wolves roam the Fairholm range near Banff, but other than their tracks and scat, they're seldom seen. They generally avoid all human contact. I'd only spotted the pack once, and only for a moment as they disappeared into the woods.

"I have them on film," he said, and he unstrapped a fancy camera. "We were hiking behind Sunshine Village, completely alone, when we saw them in the distance."

He opened a window on the camera. Sunshine Village was a ski resort, known in the summer for its magnificent wild flowers, but if you hiked to the left, as they did, toward Mount Assiniboine, you could find yourself in a vast meadow surrounded by ridges where all signs of human life disappear. A grainy image appeared on his camera. There were four animals trotting in the distance, and he was right, they were wolves.

"They're wolves alright. I can tell by their long legs." At a distance, I told him, wolves can look like a coyote or a dog, but the tell tale sign is their legs, almost disproportionately long to the rest of their body.

"Were you scared?" I asked.

"A little," his wife volunteered. "We were all by ourselves."

Rarely have wolves attacked people, but they do attack cattle and sheep, and as a result have been hunted, poisoned and trapped almost to extinction. A rancher once told me, "Modern folks have lost it, but I haven't, a sixth sense. I can tell if a wolf is lurking around. I don't even have to see it."

I was surprised the German couple only saw four wolves. The packs I'd heard about had eight to ten members. A dominant male leads the pack, with a chosen mate at his side. Strangely, it's usually only this couple that breeds, and then the pups are raised by the whole pack, the wolves taking turns looking after them while the others hunt.

People travel to Tanzania to get a glimpse of the big five: lion, rhinoceros, elephant, water buffalo and leopard. For people visiting the Canadian Rockies the big five would be the grizzly bear, the mountain lion, the wolf, the elk . . . and perhaps the tiny ground squirrel. How did the diminutive squirrel get on the list? They bite. The little hellions cause more visits to the emergency room than any of the other four. They're furry and cute, and the tourists love to feed them. Unfortunately, to the squirrel a finger looks the same as a tasty niblet.

They dig tunnels underground with holes several yards apart. And I've seen them run a hunting dog cross-eyed, beep beeping the dog from one hole to another. It's a game for both of them, and the dog never, never wins.

But I'm being churlish restricting the count to five. It's equally fascinating to spot a moose, mountain sheep, a coyote, a lynx, or if you're extremely lucky, even a wolverine. And in Banff there are experts on all of these. Connie and I went to a lecture about the wolverine. The room was packed. Wolverines apparently travel hundreds of miles, can scale a vertical mountain face in minutes, and though not much bigger than a possum, they've been known to take on a grizzly. They gnaw right though the bones, said the speaker, and they don't give up. "If you ever hear one, your hair will stand up on end . . . think of a pissed off chainsaw."

But here's the thing. Whether it's the scrapings on a tree, a beaver dam, or a vole running for cover, I was quickly discovering that living in the Rockies sensitizes you to wildlife in ways that only an untamed wilderness can. You could no more ignore it than a New Yorker could ignore the tall buildings and taxi cabs. And as you become more aware of animals and their behavior, what sets us apart as humans seems to get less and less distinct. Just watching fish and animals at play can reveal every emotion and quick-thinking strategy imaginable. Yet as more and more people live in places where their awareness diminishes that we are one tiny part of a complex multitude of species, we risk using our dominance to continue to do more harm than good.

And it seems by evidence of research that we learn more about animals' complex inter-communications every day. "We have a tendency to judge their intelligence by how we ourselves communicate instead of trying to learn their complex language," said one researcher.

Squirrels for example have different sounds in which they warn one another of a predator; one sound if the predator's simply in the area, another sound if it's threatening, and another sound if the predator's leaving, and so forth. (Incidentally, to protect their baby squirrels from predators the mother actually carries their poop off in her mouth to somewhere outside the nest so predators won't smell their whereabouts. Baby squirrels actually have to be taught how to defecate. They can't poop without being stimulated, which the mother does by licking their anuses with her tongue. Orphaned squirrels raised by humans risk becoming constipated. But please, I repeat please, should you find a baby squirrel, use a warm washcloth!).

———·———

Connie was out doing errands. The door bell rings. Two men in their thirties are standing on the stoop.

"The sign says you have vacancies?"

"Yes, yes I do," says I.

They stare at me.

I stare at them.

Now here is my predicament, my little pickle. Each of our rooms have only one queen sized bed. Women do not mind sharing a bed. They do it with frequency. They don't even bat an eye about it. Men don't. It doesn't happen. Never. Unless, of course . . . they are gay. I quickly looked for a sign, finding none. My mind began to reel. If I say, "Each of our rooms has only one bed," I lose both ways. If they're gay it sounds like I disapprove. If they're not gay it sounds like I thought they were!

Instead, I blurt, "Yes, would you like to see the rooms?" Perfect, now the rooms can do the work. Not so perfect. I wait downstairs thinking two straight men are peering into a room and wondering, "What the hell is he thinking?"

The men return downstairs. "We'll take the front room," an effeminate voice declares.

"Wonderful!" I reply, over exuberantly, suppressing the urge to exclaim, "You're gay! Of course you're gay. Now aren't we glad we got that out of the way!"

———·———

Connie opened her mail. From the look on her face something was bringing out her inner wolverine.

"What's that?"

"It's the B&B's bill from Visa and Master Card. Last year I spent over five percent of my revenues, five cents on every dollar of my hard earned income, for the privilege of doing the credit card companies' bidding."

"It really is absurd," I agreed. "Visa and Master Card didn't start out that way. But they're a monopoly now, and getting it both ways, charging the consumer onerous interest rates and fees, and the businesses that service their transactions a percentage of every sale."

"Not only that," Connie said. "I pay for the machine, I pay when I'm not even using it, and those air miles and premiums the customer is offered, I'm the one whose charged for that too!"

"If the government really wanted to stimulate the economy they'd force the credit card companies to quit charging businesses. Failing that," I said, "every retailer should announce it is no longer accepting credit cards until providing the service for the credit card companies is free. Without us they have no business. That would end the double billing in a heartbeat!"

Some B&Bs had resorted to only accepting cash, and I'd noticed some others offered a discount if the guest didn't pay with a credit card, but neither of those served the traveling visitor well. I could appreciate how Connie felt.

Connie turned on her computer, and her mood brightened. "Look! We got a nice review on Trip Advisor."

The people who posted the review mentioned the dates they stayed at the B&B, and Connie and I remembered the couple. "We arrived from England to a nice cup of tea. Connie and Jamie were the perfect hosts! Jamie's local tips were invaluable."

Connie grinned. "You've heard of the fitness celebrity, and the celebrity chef," she said. "Maybe you'll become the map celebrity!"

When it comes to technology, Connie and I are practically Amish. We're gadget impaired. But it's here that I have to admit that the internet has been a boon to the B&B keeper.

Ninety percent of our reservations and all of our confirmations take place via email. But more importantly, the internet has reduced Connie's marketing costs to comparatively nil. In the past, a B&B was dependent on expensive brochures and print advertising, which included costly reviews placed in booklets promoting escapes and romantic getaways. Today, it all boils down to a web site. Once the web site is well designed and running, it simply is a matter of assuring the B&B appears on the right links. And then it's customer reviews that become consequential. It goes without saying that reviews—from books and automobiles to restaurants and B&Bs—have been taken out of the realm of the chosen few and placed into the public domain. At least a fourth of our inquiries mention they had read about Connie's B&B on Trip Advisor.

Connie flipped through her reservation book. "I've only got a few more nights this summer to fill," she said. "And I'll probably fill those with walk-ups!"

"You've worked very hard," I said. "And from one business man to another, I'm proud of you."

She looked up and smiled, and for one brief moment she allowed a spark of pride. "Oh, what do I know about business? I just love the B&B."

Chapter 16

Gardens

"Bears . . . Shmares!." I said. "I just don't want people laughing at my funeral. Did you know that four hundred people a year around the world are killed by falling coconuts?"

"Imagine. You go to the funeral. 'Jeez, what happened to ol' Fred? He seemed like he was in such good health.'"

"He was. He got hit on the head with a coconut."

"What?" And then it starts. They can't hold it back. First a snicker. Then because of the solemnity of the occasion, a barely suppressed giggle. Someone else overhears. "A coconut?"

"Yup. He was sitting on a chaise at the beach. You know how Fred liked to read." This isn't good.

A guest at the breakfast table pipes up. "Imagine you're not killed. That's worse! You'll be hearing the giggles the rest of your life as you're wheeled around, drooling."

This is clearly a sick crowd! "Okay, now don't laugh, this is NOT funny. I read this in the obituaries this morning. Under the heading, William Pace, record holder, it says, 'William L. Pace, holder of the Guinness World Record for living the longest with a bullet in his head, died July 7th at a nursing home in Turlock, California. He was 103."

"William Lawlis Pace died 94 years and six months after his older brother accidentally shot him with their father's .22 caliber rifle in 1917. In 2006, Mr. Pace learned that he had been crowned the world record-holder in the category of unwanted cranial ammunition acquisition.'"

The conversation switched to traveling mishaps, and as it often did, the conversation flowed freely long after breakfast was finished. In the old days conversation was an art. You were invited to dinner events because of your clever eloquence, and because of your charm at being a good listener. Then, as now, when seated with others, conversation was a privilege and a social obligation. In one way or another you were expected to participate, to keep the conversation flowing.

And the B&B guests seldom fail to rise to the occasion, especially having the opportunity after days on the road to connect with others who also have a passion for travel and new places. And if the same guests stay more than one night, any first morning awkwardness is quickly replaced that evening, and the following mornings, with an easy comfort. Any conversational input by us is welcome, but rarely needed . . . except in one instance.

On a few occasions we have had young people in their twenties, unknown to one another, arrive at the B&B. "This will be nice," Connie says. "They're all the same age. They'll enjoy chattering over breakfast." Silence. Dead silence. It's torturous.

I step in to rescue them, never asking, "So how about that online social networking. How's that working out for you guys?"

———•———

It was Briana's day to help at the B&B, which gave Connie and me a chance to pack a picnic lunch and head out early to the Canmore Folk Festival. Twenty minutes east, but still in the middle of the Rockies, Canmore was an old mining town, that due to its commercial influence, had skirted Banff's "need to reside law," and its growth restrictions. As a result its population had doubled to twice the size of Banff, and it was rapidly becoming a part-time community to the wealthy from Calgary who could afford to purchase a weekend escape. And little was more popular than the annual folk festival that also had grown over the years.

We parked a few blocks from the field and bought an all-day ticket. Four stages were hosting a revolving array of talent. As Connie and I rotated during the day from one stage to another I was amazed at the level of entertainment, individuals and groups largely unknown at a national level, that had managed to craft enough of a living playing at festivals and smaller venues.

Hundreds of locals sat comfortably in the grass, some of whom danced spontaneously near the stages when the right beat struck. It was the perfect setting. The rugged mountains in the background, and the earthy garb worn by the locals and the performers alike made it seem as though nothing was out of place. Nature, the music, and a similar brand of people all blended in.

Connie and I hated to leave. We lingered at the tents selling jewelry and homemade crafts as we exited, while happily feeling the same sense of harmony. The days rolled along, sharing a sense of routine, in a treasured home in a beautiful part of the world.

———•———

"Boy, am I naïve," a guest laughed, as he took a seat at the breakfast table. "We just paid forty dollars for a tour last night called Wildlife Safari. It took us around the Minnewanka loop, and exactly where we'd followed your same directions yesterday!"

I chuckled in empathy, for he triggered a recent memory. "Don't feel bad," I said. "I was in Thailand a few years ago and signed up for an excursion to meet the famous and reclusive hill people. There were eight of us, including the guide, and a nice Canadian couple."

"We took off early in the morning with a bus ride that took us to an elephant camp where we were loaded onto the backs of the elephants. We then jostled up and down and sideways through the jungle for an hour. The elephants finally stopped at a river's edge where we traveled by dugout on a muddy, twisting river with tall reeds on either bank. Then we stopped, and got out, and began arduously hiking through the forest. At one point a bird shrieked."

"'What's that?' the Canadian girl asked me."

"Apes," I said. "Thai gorillas."

"She thought for a minute, and I grinned. 'Okay,' she said, 'Canadians are naïve.'"

"We kept hiking. It must have been for two hours. Some of the Europeans, winded, stopped by the side of the trail for a rest. Finally, we walked over a ridge. There it was! At first a few wooden sheds with chickens strutting about, then a hut, and then there they were! Two teenage girls, some older women, and a few men, all dressed in strange, brightly colored apparel with beads and rings on their necks and ankles."

"They were sitting in front of a table of trinkets next to a cooler of soft drinks. 'Drinks for everyone,' I shouted, so overcome with meeting this remote tribe in the middle of nowhere that I bought several trinkets. Finally, the guide said, 'It's time to go.'"

"We walked twenty yards, emerging out of the trees. And the two teenage girls suddenly flew past me on a motor scooter, smiling and waving a friendly goodbye. And there below sat our bus beside a busy two lane highway."

"As I climbed on the bus, the Canadian girl laughed, 'I guess Canadians aren't the only ones who are naïve.'"

———•———

A king, so it goes, had sent out a scribe to concoct the perfect dessert. Not too hot. Not too cold. Not too sweet. Not too bold. And so was invented the incomparable hot fudge sundae. If he'd asked for the perfect weather I feel certain he'd have been served a Banff summer day.

Connie was looking radiant in a light summer dress. "The grass feels so soft on my bare feet," she smiled. "Come on let's see how the garden is doing."

We strolled over to a corner of the yard where Connie had fashioned a nice triangle out of the grass. Amidst the brown soil, rows of neatly lined vegetables were starting to show. "Look," she said, "the lettuce is green and leafy, and those are carrots and peas starting to grow!"

As we admired her garden I couldn't help noticing an aroma emanating from the flowers she had planted. A sweet scent from the hyacinth and the daffodils left a marvelous fragrance in the air. "Just wait until the lilacs bloom," Connie said, as I lightly touched petals surrounding an apricot-orange cup next to a flower with creamy white petals. A few bumble bees hovered around their newfound paradise.

Connie and I noticed four guests had come out and were chatting comfortably on the back deck. We had a sense of what the guests derived from the B&B. For them it was a little bit of everything—the maps, the other guests, a welcoming home, and the chance to be among locals. But for Connie and me, it was something else. Something magical. I'd always imagined living in a pre-television time, a Gatsby era, when people had interesting conversations without glancing at their watches—at breakfast, over tea, or in the evenings with the lights reflecting off their brandy glasses.

That world still existed, but only among fellow travelers, and for Connie and I, it flourished here at her B&B. It didn't really matter if we participated, though sometimes we happily did; it was simply just nice to see. It was another world, a special unhurried world, and Connie and I adored it.

"I think I'll see if they'd like some lemonade," Connie smiled.

As we walked toward the house the phone rang.

"I'll get it," I said.

I stepped from the bedroom into the kitchen. Connie was arranging some cookies on a plate. "They'll like these!" she said.

"It's for you," I said, and I handed her the phone.

"Hello," she said, and her voice grew softer. "I see," she said, "of course."

Connie's face had suddenly lost its color. "Who was that?" I asked.

"It was the real estate agent. There is a young couple who would like to come by and see the house."

Connie served the cookies and lemonade, and we went outside for a walk. She didn't talk about it, there wasn't much to say, but a quiet had enveloped her that nothing in the moment could erase.

Connie didn't say much the whole evening. We went to bed early, and arose at dawn, an hour ahead of the guests. Connie looked out the kitchen window. "Oh, no!" she cried, and she ran into the back yard, "Look what the deer have done! They've eaten all the lettuce, and the buds off half the flowers." Her eyes filled with tears. Then she fell onto her knees beside her garden. "I worked so hard...don't they know how hard I worked," and she began to cry. I held her in my arms as tears flowed down her cheeks.

Chapter 17
Ebony Sculptures

Whether we liked it or not we had been jolted back into reality. The couple, it turns out, wasn't a serious buyer, but eventually there would be, and there simply wasn't any way to prepare for it. All we could do was appreciate the time in the B&B we had.

But as the days went by, and there were no new buyers on the horizon, we drifted back into our routine as though we'd been given some invisible reprieve.

———•———

Connie lay sprawled on a blanket, resting, on a secluded hillside we frequented on Johnson Lake. If I looked out beyond the trees, I would see water, the beach, the children, the blue sky. To the right, teenagers had claimed a flat, grassy area. Across from them I could hear distant shrieks from their intrepid friends swinging from a rope into the frigid waters—the same screams of painful delight that the hermit of Inglismaldie must have heard decades earlier.

This spot that we'd come to think of as ours, where we'd often come to read in the afternoons, was much like the B&B; behind us was the quietude of a spring Monet, while in front were all the colors and gaiety of a Toulouse Lautrec.

But there was something profoundly different about our view from only a week ago, and with binoculars I could still see tiny plumes of smoke rising from the ground where a verdant, green forest had been. The pungent smell of the smoke still permeated the air.

A week earlier, the sky behind Johnson Lake, above Rundle Mountain, was a crimson red with streaks of yellow, not too dissimilar from the fires that raged beneath, scorching the earth in a windblown rush of destruction.

The week before had started with a veil of white smoke that had descended over the valley, smoke from fires as far away as Washington and Oregon. Warning signs for a month had been posted, alerting visitors to be especially careful, that this was a particularly dry summer. And then a bolt of lightning, or something as simple as a camp fire left smoldering, ignited a string of devastating fires along Route 1, and Route 93 near Marble Canyon toward Radium. Thousands of acres were in flames. Between prescribed burns intentionally set to try to draw a defensive line, and wind-carried sparks that lifted the fires across rivers and highways, no one could tell anymore where it even started.

For days, as helicopters flew overhead with giant buckets of water, ashes fell from the sky, and if you accidentally opened a window you were quickly enveloped in smoke. From your car you could see the flames devouring the forest floor, climbing rapidly up the trees. The Trans-Canada highway was still open, which under the circumstances, was only slightly better than observing it closed. The town of Kelowna, a half day's drive from Banff, had been evacuated when the same string of fires burst though their defenses and burned several neighborhoods to the ground.

Peering through my binoculars to the east it was amazing to see whole mountain sides of blackened trees, riveting ebony sculptures recast into jagged pieces of modern art, while in other places small patches were scorched in the middle of an untouched forest. And where we sat it was still lush and green, as though nothing had happened.

Connie and I had circled the lake with a park ranger only a few weeks prior. "How would you rate that forest over there in terms of its health?" the ranger asked the group, pointing to a rich flank in the valley covered with pines, trees now charred to the blackest black that I'd ever seen. On a scale of one to ten several people in the group proffered an eight or a nine.

"I'd give it a six," he said. "You have to look below the surface to see what condition a forest is really in. A healthy forest has to have ground, herbaceous, shrub and canopy. The trees you're looking at are packed tightly together. They're all the same height, competing for sunlight, and little underneath can grow. So how do you get it back? You burn it down. Forest fires are the giver of life."

I doubt if he could have predicted the speed in which his comments had become so prophetic. But I had hiked through charred forests and it's true; given time, something wondrous happens. Seeds released from the burning trees begin sprouting millions of tiny saplings in varying stages of growth amidst wild flowers—purple fireweed and bright red Indian paint brushes and daisys as far as the eye can see—all carpeting the soil under the stark black sculptures, framing the landscape in an eerie, yet beautiful display of the old versus the new.

Wildlife begins to help. Squirrels spread the seeds. Camouflaged against the deep black trees the black-backed woodpecker digs out wood-boring insect larvae from the dead trees. In fact, burned forests are essential to the survival of many wildlife species. "It can take over thirty years," the ranger said, "for a forest to regenerate, which in nature's time is merely the blink of an eye."

Connie stirred. "What's that?" she asked, and she pointed to something large swimming in the water.

We didn't have any check-ins, and we'd allowed ourselves time to see the dusk slowly settle over the lake. Only a few people were still there.

"I'm going to have a closer look! Whatever it is, it's huge!" Connie said, and she leapt to her feet and ran to a bank above the lake, with me following close behind. "I think it's an otter!"

"An otter? Are there otters here?" I said.

"Well, it's too big to be a beaver. It must be five feet long from head to tail." Just then its tail splashed the water, and it began swimming in another direction. A dog saw it and began barking wildly.

"Darn," she said, "I'd never seen an otter!"

We skirted along the edge, gleaning a closer look. It was truly a magnificent animal, sliding through the glassy water, disappearing, and reappearing where we least expected it. Finally, still excited from the surprise encounter, we gathered our things, and climbed toward the parking lot. When we got to the top of the hill we ran into a fisherman. Now this was no ordinary fisherman. He'd fished these parts for years. With a smile, and a crinkle around his eyes, and backwoods wisdom to spare, he was the kind of man with whom you'd love to spend the day.

I approached him with Connie at my side. "We just saw a large brown animal gliding in the water. Do you know what it is?"

"Did it slap the water with its tail?"

"Yes!" Connie replied. "I think it's an otter."

"It's a beaver."

Connie's face began scrooching up.

"Thank you," I said, and we walked toward the car, with me in utter amusement, for Connie has a problem not uncommon to her species. She hates, absolutely *hates*, admitting she is wrong. If you pinched her cheeks in hopes she could form the word, all that would squeak out would be, "waw . . . waw."

We got in the car and drove away in silence. I didn't say a word; I knew this was killing her. Nor did she. We were halfway home before she finally spoke. The words came out almost in a whisper, "I still think it was an otter."

When we got home I quietly looked up otter in the encyclopedia. It turns out an otter is an all encompassing name for any of thirteen semi-aquatic mammals who feed on fish, usually have brown fur and flat tails, and include among weasels and wolverines . . . the beaver. So there you have it. She was right and the fisherman was wrong. He was right and she was wrong. And only in Canada do two wrongs make a right!

———·———

I picked up the *Outlook*. On page three was an announcement that caught my attention. Tomorrow would be the first annual memorial walk for Isabelle Dube, organized by her husband and a circle of friends. A local school teacher, mother of one, and only thirty-six years old, Isabelle had been killed the previous summer by a grizzly bear. This isn't Disneyland.

Chapter 18

This is not Disneyland

The Silvertip Golf Course had been built, not without controversy, on a high ridge overlooking Canmore. As with most golf course developments it was a prelude to lucrative real estate transactions with partners brought in to develop residential communities along its boundaries.

Wildlife conservationists were of course up in arms. It was one more example of a wildlife corridor being carved up for human use. But the conservationists didn't have the same protections afforded their counterparts in Banff. A thriving mining community until well into the 1950s, though only minutes from Banff, Canmore, as mentioned earlier, had evaded the development restrictions that preserved the area surrounding Banff. As a result the Trans-Canada Highway divided Canmore in half, leaving a downtown core and small town feel harder to discern, while housing developments had crept up the sides of mountains in all directions, some right in the middle of fire prone forests.

What Isabelle Dube didn't know, jogging that afternoon with two friends on a path near the golf course, was that only minutes before, golf course employees had chased a four-year-old grizzly off the fairway, driving the bear out from behind a speeding, honking, motorized cart.

This was the bear's territory. And it was agitated. Agitated to the point that when Isabelle and her two friends rounded the corner it instinctively reacted.

For some reason, instead of remaining close to her friends, Isabelle, an athletic mountain biker, panicked and climbed a tree. The grizzly singled her out and quickly pulled her down. Within minutes Isabelle was dead. When the Park officials arrived the grizzly was still hovering near her body. They shot and destroyed the bear. This isn't Disneyland.

Having lived in the city I'd grown somewhat inured to the deaths of people from car accidents, senseless crime, and cancer killing diseases. What I wasn't prepared for, and can never be, are the deaths in the Canadian Rockies of people in the prime of their lives, out having fun, who in the moment make the wrong decision.

It's easy to see how it happens. Modern clothing and gadgetry give the impression we aren't as vulnerable to nature as we once were, coupled with Hollywood and extreme sports that have promoted risks outside the bounds of common sense. And added to that is a feeling tourists have that because they are on holiday they are immune to danger, that the normal risks don't apply.

Connie and I vacationed in Kauai earlier in the year. Signs everywhere warned of riptides, advise we heeded having come from a tourist town, and also advised "Never turn your back on the ocean," a warning that didn't hit me as all that threatening until I ran into an orthopedic surgeon who lived on the island. "I've only been here a year," he said, "and already I've seen three cases. Couples are here on their honeymoon. One is in the water up to their waist and the other hollers out to turn around and pose for a picture. A wave comes from behind, lifts him up and drives him onto his head in the hard sand. The next thing their spouse knows they are married to a paraplegic." In the Canadian Rockies one can multiply the risks tenfold. And it isn't just the tourists who get hurt or killed; often it's locals, sports and mountaineering experts who have grown too complacent and sure of themselves.

A well experienced local climber in his early thirties joined a companion for a morning of rock climbing. It's a sport popular in the Canadian Rockies. There are schools and guides, and the certified climber was considered to be one of the best of them. With ropes and clamps attached to their waists they strolled up a three-foot ledge, ascending to the place where their climb would begin. The ledge still had a thin layer of snow. The climber was following behind. He suddenly slipped on an icy patch, landed on his back, gained momentum and slid off the ledge, falling thirty meters. He died of massive head injuries, his helmet offering little protection.

An avalanche comes rushing down at over two hundred miles per hour, producing winds so powerful that trees along its path are uprooted. Massive chunks of snow crystallize as it tumbles, propelling a cloud of icy particles out front like a gaseous blast, blinding anyone caught in its ferocity. Your only hope is to try to swim on its surface. Caught underneath is being buried in packed snow the weight of cement. You can't move. You can't breathe.

How do avalanches happen? As a sign near an avalanche chute succinctly describes it, "The steep slopes accumulate layer upon layer of snow. New snowfalls compress previous layers into ice. Warm Chinook winds create sudden thaws that can cause the fresh layers to slide off the frozen crusts." But the odds of simply being in the wrong place at the wrong time are miniscule. What the sign doesn't say is that more often than not, when people are caught in an avalanche, they had a hand in triggering it.

West of Banff, outside the park, eight snowmobilers set off for the back country. They had known each other since childhood, and they'd done this countless times, racing their snowmobiles up the side of a steep mountain, seeing how high they could go before circling around and speeding back down. None returned home this time. I suspect as a safety precaution some had signal emitters to help locate them should they become buried under the snow. But that would have required someone else still alive to hear it.

Two young snowboarders from out of town were more fortunate. After skiing out of bounds at Sunshine Ski resort in search of fresh powder, they found themselves trapped on a ledge high on a precipice halfway down the mountain. One had a cell phone, and luckily where they were, they still had cell phone reception. Otherwise, they'd still be there. As it was they spent two cold and terrifying nights clinging to the edge.

Rescuers first tried to use a helicopter for a long-line rescue, but violent winds forced the helicopter to return. The rescue team next tried to ski above the boarders, but fears of triggering an avalanche aborted that attempt as well. The next day the weather was worse, more snow and fierce winds, which again meant no attempt. Finally, rescuers were able to climb up to them and lower them by ropes to an area safely accessible by air.

Lest one thinks these are rare and isolated incidents, the rescue teams were called out over a hundred times last year alone. The Canadian rescue teams are so experienced that other countries have requested their services more than once in perilous situations.

An experienced ice climber traversing the foot of Johnston Canyon in order to scale the vertical sheets of ice on the other side stepped through a snow bridge and found himself downriver under the ice, a river of water streaming beneath him. Hikers above could see him under the ice trying to crack the thick slab with his ice axe, to no avail. Knowing he only had a few minutes, he remembered a clear spot about twenty yards downstream and frantically swam for the opening. He popped up, wet and frozen, relieved to be shuffled away alive in warm blankets.

A fifty-three-year-old woman, in excellent condition, was found deceased in the snow less than forty yards from a snow packed road, a road she never saw. She had gone out snowshoeing, alone, following the beauty of the fresh snow. But a sudden heavy snowfall obliterated her tracks. She got disoriented and froze to death walking in circles.

The spring and summer bring even more mishaps. One of the saddest involved a young couple and their six year old son relaxing near the river by Banff's central park. The river was still covered in ice, but recent temperatures, unknown to the couple, had been warm. The little boy playfully rushed onto the ice. The father quickly went after him. The boy ran back, but the ice broke under his father's weight. Others nearby raced to his rescue, forming a line on their stomachs, trying desperately to save him, but his clothes and his panicked struggle dragged him under. Tragically, ten yards down the river from where he drowned he could have stood in shallow water no higher than his waist.

A thirty-year-old biking enthusiast, touring the Icefields Parkway with his girlfriend, stopped at Bow Lake and rented a kayak. His girlfriend stayed on shore. Fed by Bow glacier, the lake is nearly a mile wide. He paddled to the very middle. A sudden squall came up, and the gusting winds capsized his boat. He probably had a life preserver, but he wasn't wearing it. Far from shore, in the middle of a torrential rain, it wouldn't have mattered. The temperature of the water was barely above freezing. He sank to the bottom of the lake, as frozen bodies do, while his girlfriend paced anxiously, waiting for his return.

Young men like to scramble up the rock faces with no ropes and little training. A twenty-three year-old lost his life last month doing exactly that. And then there was the couple hiking behind Rundle Mountain. The trails to the summit are precarious enough, but they found themselves hiking on a dangerous path, off the main trail. One of them must have slipped while the other tried to grab them, for both of their bodies were found a hundred feet below on the rocks. There isn't enough money to want to trade places with the park rangers having to call the parents of these three young people recently embarked on a fun holiday.

If the wardens know that there is bear activity in the area, they often post signs suggesting that you hike in a party of six. Such signs are often posted around Minnewanka Lake where a sow and her cubs are known to frequent. It didn't stop one hiker, a woman hiking alone, pictured the next day in the newspaper being loaded into an ambulance on a stretcher, her face streaked in blood from a scalp wound.

Tourists who come to the Rockies for a short visit seldom hear such stories, but when you live here the incidents accumulate. I often tell young people staying at the B&B to follow their instincts; if it feels dangerous just don't do it! Yet there doesn't seem to be a limit to tourists who send their children out of the car for a closer look at the mountain sheep, animals with horns that can easily dent a fender, or visitors who crowd around a huge elk in order to snap a picture. These animals aren't house pets. Like the natural surroundings, they don't necessarily growl or give a warning, they just suddenly react. When that happens you're quickly reminded that this is not Disneyland.

Chapter 19

Introverts and Extroverts . . .
and Little Lambs Eat Ivy

People can't resist asking, "Are there bad guests? I mean guests you can't . . . well, you know?"

That's a good question. Hell, it's a question I'd want to ask. So here's the answer. Rarely. Very, very, rarely. Ninety eight percent of the guests we thoroughly enjoy. Not infrequently we are sad when they leave, wishing that they lived nearby. And even if a traveler arrives on edge, rattled and a bit testy, we take it as a challenge to calm their ruffled soul; we nice them into submission.

BUT, and here's the scandalous truth, every now and then, rarely, very rarely, we'll get someone excessively needy. Someone who needs, needs, needs, *attention*.

Sometimes it's a couple. "Oh my God. They've sucked the life out of each other, and now they're trying to do it to us!" I wail.

But usually it's someone traveling alone. You can spot it before they even arrive, cringing from their multiple emails. A case in point was a middle aged woman from England.

"Oh dear, can you tell me where I can get a pair of slippers? How far is that? Is there anywhere else? Will they cost very much?'

Moments later. "Can you help me get this camera back in its case? Here, you might need to read the instructions."

Followed by, "Would you go over the bus schedule one more time? Do you think I should take my backpack or leave it here?'

Later that night there is a knock on our bedroom door.

"You answer it."

"No, you."

"No, you."

I begin to weep, a broken man. "Please . . . I just can't take it anymore."

But I've only lost it with a guest once, and I'm chagrined to say it happened only recently. No, it wasn't with Kimono lady who asked to change rooms three times, nor was it with the California scriptwriter who woke me up in the middle of the night asking me if I could hear the low frequency—him, I could understand. No, I lost it with Ishmael. And I regret it deeply . . . kinda.

Ishmael is a short man, with a kind face, and a soft but steadfast composure. There were three retired couples traveling together, and Ishmael had been elected their spokesman, partly because he had better command of the language, but mostly because poor Ishmael had made all the arrangements.

Connie and I knew we were in trouble when one of the ladies arrived with five suitcases and then began complaining that the room was too small, not to us in English, but in sweeping arm motions to her wilting husband. After Banff, they had booked themselves on a cruise ship heading up the Alaskan straits. "Wait til she gets a load of that room. The captain will be tossing the bags overboard," I whispered to Connie.

They soon wiped the smile off my face. All six assembled for Connie's welcome in the living room. Connie went over everything and then asked if there were any allergies, or any foods they didn't eat. Ishmael just smiled. Everything was fine. But instead of the fruit dish Connie always prepares for breakfast one of the ladies asked, "Would it be possible to have a plate of vegetables instead?"

"What did you have in mind?" Connie asked, whereupon the woman itemized a list of tomatoes, red peppers, onions, green beans and three other items.

Connie, ever amenable, looked at her watch, and said, "Of course."

It was nine o'clock. We didn't have half the things she petitioned so Connie walked down to Safeway, and picked out each and every item, while I stored the extra suitcases. She then returned and made five nutritious fruit plates and one oddly exacting vegetable plate.

I told Connie to sleep in the next morning. I would cook and serve breakfast. We both felt the guest wanted something different just for the sake of being treated special. Perhaps it was why when Ishmael asked me to warm his milk in the microwave prior to each and every time he poured it into his coffee, while I was juggling a full breakfast, that I began to feel annoyed.

They ate everything. And then they sat quietly, comfortably at the table, while Ishmael asked me to come over.

"Yes Ishmael?"

"We were wondering," he said, "if for breakfast from now on we could all have a vegetable plate like hers?"

I suddenly blurted, "Ishmael. This is not a restaurant. It's a B&B, we don't have a menu! We cook a hearty basic Canadian breakfast."

They shuffled up to their rooms and I thought, Uh oh, this isn't going to look good on Trip Advisor. I was thinking of Connie trudging last night to Safeway, and piqued, I may have just harmed her B&B. I was relieved when instead of feeling insulted, Ishmael sidled up to me later that morning, and said, "I am sorry. We sometimes forget that we didn't travel all the way here to mirror what we do in our own country."

The others came down. I smiled. They smiled. And all was well again at the Banff Avenue B&B.

————•————

The following is the googled online definition of an extrovert:

"Most people believe that an extrovert is a person who is friendly and outgoing. While that may be true, that is not the true meaning of extroversion. An extrovert is a person who is energized by being around other people. This is the opposite of an introvert who is energized by being alone.

"Extroverts tend to 'fade' when alone and can easily become bored without other people around. When given the chance, an extrovert will talk with someone else rather than sit alone and think. In fact, extroverts tend to think as they speak, unlike introverts who are far more likely to think before they speak. Extroverts often think best when they are talking. Concepts just don't seem real to them unless they can talk about them; reflecting on them isn't enough."

"Extroverts, sixty percent of the population, enjoy social situations and seek them out. Their ability to make small talk makes them appear more socially adept than introverts; although introverts may have little difficulty talking to people they don't know if they can talk about ideas or issues."

"Extrovert behavior seems to be the standard in American society, in which other behavior is judged. However, extroverted behavior is simply a manifestation of the way an extrovert interacts with the world. Extroverts are interested in and concerned with the external world."

The following is the googled online definition of an introvert:

"Contrary to what most people think, an introvert is not simply a person who is shy or reserved. In fact, being shy has little to do with being an introvert! Shyness has an element of apprehension, nervousness and anxiety, and while an introvert may also be shy, introversion is not shyness. An introvert is a person who is energized by being alone and whose energy is drained by being around other people."

"Introverts are more concerned with the inner world of the mind. They enjoy thinking, and exploring their inner thoughts and feelings. They often avoid social situations because being around people drains their energy. This is true even if they have excellent social skills. After being with people any length of time, such as a party, they need time alone to recharge."

"When introverts want to be alone, it is not a sign of being withdrawn or low spirits. It means that they either need to regain their energy from being around other people or that they simply want the time to be alone with their own thoughts. Being with people, even people they are comfortable with, can prevent them from their desire to be quietly introspective."

"Being introspective, though, doesn't mean that an introvert doesn't enjoy conversations. However, those conversations are generally about ideas and concepts, not what they consider the trivial matters of small talk."

Connie and I are introverts. On a one to ten scale, introvert to extrovert, we are a 3.5 (Okay, a 3.7 if you throw in some volleyball).

Why does this matter? Wouldn't the environment of a B&B be perfect, small groups of people, often one-on-one, enjoying subjects of consequence? Absolutely. But I liken it to waking up affixed to a canister. An extrovert's canister is empty and during the day, helped immeasurably by today's cell phones and constant connectivity, the canister fills up with energy. Add in a party or two and by nightfall it's positively brimming. Connie and I awake with a full canister, quietly enjoying our coffee, allowing the newspaper to spark stimulating inner reflections. With each encounter, enjoyable though it may be, our canisters slowly empty. By the end of the day, if we don't moderate our social interactions, our canisters are empty. The canister fills back up, but each day it starts out a little less full. Until one morning you wake up, and you can't even find the canister. You're exhausted. Spent. Not an ounce of energy left. The thought of even seeing the mailman, let alone an inquisitive B&B guest, is unnerving.

And the problem is that you can't see it coming. The days are long, and make no mistake about it, I help, but helping isn't the same as being ultimately responsible. The hours are pleasant and rewarding, yet we are always *on*, and we notice it when we periodically have no guests. The house is empty and our bodies suddenly relax, every inch seeming to shed some unseen weight we didn't even know we were carrying.

It was mid-summer and we hit the wall at the same time. Connie hadn't stopped for a minute, from teaching to immediately running the B&B. And after a thirty-five-hundred-mile drive, I'd run the B&B through June and hadn't had a rest since, either. We were worn out. We needed to refill our canisters. Thank God we had each other.

"You go first," I insisted. "You've been wanting to visit your sister. Take off for four or five days, and then I'll go somewhere when you return. Briana will be here to help a few of the days you're gone."

"Would you like my mother to come down and give you a hand?"

"Noooooo."

"Why not?"

"I scare. I scare."

A change can be as good as a rest. While Connie was away I browsed through some Alberta travel guides. Luxury retreat? No, not for me. Backwoods cabin? Too desolate. Fishing camp? Boring.

And then, there it was. I found my escape. Skyline Ranch. Nestled in the Porcupine Hills in southern Alberta, cowboy country, it was a working ranch with cattle and horseback riding. I began to feel my canister fill up . . .

And before I knew it I was washing the dishes and singing a little ditty.

"*Mairzy doats and dozy doats and liddle lamzy divey*
A kiddley divey too, wouldn't you".

"*If the words sound queer and funny to your ear, a little bit jumbled and jivey,*
Sing mares eat oats and does eat oats and little lambs eat ivy."

"*A kid'll eat ivy too, wouldn't you*"

Chapter 20
Beyond the Hills

Suddenly, a man I liked, a man I admired, a type of man fast fading from the western landscape, was on the ground on his knees, in a life or death situation . . . and there wasn't a damn thing I could do about it! But I'm getting ahead of the story.

———•———

As I drive toward the ranch, the wilderness changes. The mountains turn lighter in color, patched in bright blotches of brown and orange, mesmerizing before ending abruptly. Cattle begin to appear by the road as the Kananaskis River twists its way through grassy hills.

My mind wanders to a story I remember about an internatioanally acclaimed South American poet and a journalist. Inside the corridors of a national newspaper, the poet was greeted by an enthusiastic journalist. "When I was a young man we met," said the journalist. "You were doing an interview for the magazine where I worked and I led you down the hall for the interview! Do you remember?"

The poet looked up at the journalist, and said, "I am an old man and my brain is now feeble, but in that moment my life was in your hands, and I am certain I recorded it in my heart." I smiled at the thought of that.

Alone, and at a distance, I began to reflect on things with a bit more clarity, ruminate on some things that intrigue and interest me, and try to make sense of a few things that happily confuse me. One of the nicest compliments Connie and I ever received was a comment from an elderly man who had stayed a few days at the B&B, "Connie and you clearly enjoy each others' company," he said, "and that's nice to be around."

It was a compliment I could accept, and delight in, because for me it rang true. And how nice it was, I thought, that our day-to-day interaction had a pleasurable impact on someone else's spirits.

But whereas this gentle man's poignant observation made us feel gratified and full, other words of praise and affection sometimes left us bewildered. "What did we do to deserve that?"

"Did you spend much time with them?"

"No, did you?"

"Not really."

"So in other words, the less they see of us the more they like us."

"Exactly!'

At times I felt like I was back in high school and was suddenly one of the popular kids, projecting something—God knows what—that others found attractive. Connie and I would look at our guest book and be thrilled by the comments that celebrated our virtues as hosts. Such positive reinforcement doesn't accompany most businesses, and it was a benefit I hadn't expected. But what struck me as odd, for it went beyond the unexpected niceties, was how often guests, upon leaving, would insist that we visit if anywhere near, and at least in the moment, they sincerely meant it. What could be a nicer sentiment than that, I thought. But why? What was it about the B&B, who we were and who we weren't, what we did and what we didn't do, that brought such a warm and surprising response?

And the truth is that whatever we do comes naturally, enjoyably. But what the guests see isn't completely us. What they see is the *best* of us. And the best of who we are, in this rarefied dynamic, taps into some human need, I think, that transcends age, material possessions, race and nationality. It's a need we all have and never lose: to feel that we *matter*, not for the clothes we wear, the car we drive, the position we hold, or what we've accomplished, but matter just simply for who we are.

When I would travel through third world countries I would pick up dozens of pens and pads of paper. When children would gather around I'd give each a pad and pen. The delight on their faces would shock a western child. But I'd take it another step. I'd ask each of the children to write their names on a piece of paper "so that I could always remember this moment." A calm would replace the earlier jubilation, and as they carefully wrote their names and I'd ask their help in pronouncing them, what became far more important than a pad and a pen was a sense I was trying to impart that they mattered. That I am you, and you are me. It's amazing how little we need to give, and how little we need to receive . . . to mean a lot.

Now I'm aware that it's a mighty big stretch to compare our well-to-do guests vacationing at the B&B to African children in a destitute country who no doubt feel diminished by their poverty. But nevertheless, what Connie and I do has an unintended element of consistent, simple kindness. We smile warmly at our guests, happy to see them; we point out things to do that will heighten their experience; we ask them with genuine interest about their day; we avoid controversial subjects, keeping our soapboxes stashed under our bed; we try to be friendly without being intrusive. And in the tiniest ways imaginable, whenever we encounter our guests, with little knowledge of their worldly identities, we convey that to us, while you're here, you very much *matter*.

Travelers are less guarded and more open to being open than they normally would be; feelings unfold at a more rapid pace. And all of this is accentuated by the fact that for most of our guests we are the only locals that they get to know. In certain ways we become as much a part of their travel experience as their hike up Sulfur Mountain, or their rafting trip down the Kicking Horse River.

And what makes us appear special is largely that we're *different*. To many, we represent another culture, and to all, we simply *belong*, seductively familiar in our surroundings, among visitors who are not, and that in itself is an unearned, attractive trait. But for Connie and I our lives unfold, from one guest to another, like theirs—very much in the moment. And the B&B, for guest and host, somehow brings out the best in us.

As I drove through Longview, a cattlemen's crossroads if ever there was, I remained perplexed. All that said, I still wasn't sure why guests would want us to visit them. I'd have to think about that a bit more. I pulled over for a cold Coke, and glanced at the map. The ranch was only two hours away.

———•———

I veered left off the main highway onto a gravel road. "Thirty miles," the directions noted, "before turning again at a marker beside the road." Occasionally a pick-up truck would pass, kicking up clouds of dust so thick you could taste it if you didn't roll up your window. My eyes began to feel scratchy. The dust made me think of the great cattle drives. No place, I decided, for contact lenses.

I finally spotted the small white marker with a faded arrow pointing toward Skyline Ranch. The hills now were steeper, covered in lush green grass, with pine trees darkening the hillsides amid outcroppings of rock. It was beautiful; exactly what I'd hoped to find.

Over a rise I spotted the ranch. A simple home, nothing fancy, with an addition made out of timber. The home was casting a shadow over a pond. A few RV campers were nestled by a creek, and behind the house was a corral settled in by horses.

A black and white dog yappily led the way as I turned down a bumpy dirt road. A man was outside on a tractor when I rolled to a stop. He was wearing a well worn cowboy hat.

"Just park anywhere," he said. "I'm Bill. Welcome."

Bill, I surmised, was the owner of the ranch. He appeared to be nearing seventy. And I immediately drew an impression. This was the real deal. It's the chin, I reflected. It's all in the jaw. Have you ever seen a cowboy with a weak chin? And the mustache. Nothing too trimmed. A big, bushy mustache squaring the jaw, under high cheek bones and angular features. Cowboys don't hedge their glances. They look you straight in the eye. That was my vision of a cowboy. And this was Bill in aces and spades.

"Don't mind the dog," Bill smiled. "She helps me round up the cattle. Bring in your stuff and we'll get you fixed up."

Bill opened the front door. Inside, muddy cowboy boots and shoes lined the entry way. "That's my part of the house," he said, and he pointed to the log room attachment. "This is the kitchen. I hope you like cowboy coffee. I make it myself. The grounds sink right to the bottom!"

We walked through a neatly kept dining room. "Just pick any of the rooms upstairs except for the one on the left."

"Is there anyone else staying here this week?" I asked.

"Just a young French boy. He's been working with me on the ranch. He wants to be a cowboy."

I could tell the boy wasn't in for an easy time. Bill didn't look very easy to please. Over the course of the day I gradually met the rest of the family. It was an interesting constellation. Erin arrived with two raucous boys. Erin was Bill's thirty-something daughter. A dark haired woman, easy to like, she had years earlier been named the Calgary Stampede Queen. Her husband, she said, worked for an engine repair company. Her mannerisms were pleasantly unguarded. "We live in that RV nearest the creek," she said. "But we're building a home over the hill out of sight of the ranch."

A young woman named Heather strolled in. She was married to Bill's son, a former rodeo rider. "Are you ready for your first ride?" she asked.

"I think I'll wait until tomorrow after breakfast," I replied. "If that's okay with you."

I returned upstairs and looked around. The room was simply furnished. One bathroom served the guests, with a claw foot porcelain tub. In the hall I noticed a younger picture of Bill, dressed in a Mountie uniform, standing beside a smiling woman in a wedding dress.

I wandered outside for a walk before dinner. A truck pulled up, heading in the same direction. "Get in," Bill said. "I'll show you around."

We drove a mile or so through a second gate where another corral stood. There were two cabins, and a large tent standing with what appeared to be the aftermath of a party. "Sometimes we host group events back here," he said, and I noticed the grass tamped down from recent campers. "We rent out the cabins to hunters that are here for a longer stay."

"How long have you owned the ranch?"

"My wife and I bought several hundred acres about thirty years ago. It looks bigger than what it is. All the surrounding land is free range, leased by me and other ranchers from the government."

Bill told me he had three hundred head of cattle, scattered above in the hills. "I'd hoped to just handle the horses now with my wife," he said, "and then turn the rest of the operation over to the kids. Our plan was to move back here to one of the cabins. Like me, she loved horses. Plans change though," he said. "She died of cancer two years ago unexpectedly. She was only in her early sixties." His voice trailed off, almost to a whisper, speaking more to himself than me.

We drove back in silence until Bill felt again like talking. "After my early years as a mountie my wife and I ran the ranch full time. We had more cattle back then but beef prices changed almost daily. During the summers we began opening it up to guests. And in the winters we'd fly up to the Yukon and the Northwest Territories where we'd run a camp, and I'd take hunting expeditions out for brown bear and big horned sheep."

It was almost dark by the time we returned to the ranch. That night I opened the bedroom window. Other than the sound of the wind, it was quiet. I slept soundly and awoke feeling more refreshed then I'd felt in days.

After breakfast I followed Heather to the corral. Bill had already saddled eight horses for a group of day trippers he was guiding. Heather bridled two other horses, and we trotted off in a different direction. Heather and I leaned forward as we ascended a hill to the top of a ridge. Below, I caught a glimpse of Bill, the lone cowboy, leading his group along a western meadow. I thought of the cowboy code. "Don't speak unless you have something worthy to say," and "Don't tell the trail boss he's wrong. If he is, he'll figure it out sooner or later on his own." No coincidence, I mused, that Washington's politicians felt more at home in the east.

Traveling by horseback, I decided, is the way to see the west. I trailed behind Heather, jostling along, taking in the pleasant views. Heather had been a competitive gymnast, only to miss the Nationals by being sidelined from nagging injuries. But now it appeared her struggles centered around being a newlywed. "Do you have any advice for a good marriage?" she asked casually. Though her question was broached nonchalantly, I suspected she'd like a serious answer. Things might not have been going as smoothly as she hoped.

I laughed and replied, "I'm the last person to ask about that. I always told my girlfriends to set the bar low, and they wouldn't be disappointed!"

Heather laughed, but I was trying to segue into something important, a thought about expectations, and something about men. "Be a little easy on yourself. You can have it *all*. You just can't have it all at the same time. I'm no expert on relationships," I continued, "but I do know a little about men. Women don't realize how much we need their approval. If you give it, and give it generously, we'll be there forever, helping you in any way we can. But do the opposite and we slowly feel beaten down. We lose all interest, and eventually the partnership fails, whether we stay in the relationship or not."

Heather was silent. I could tell she was thinking about what I said. "That's good advice. I'm going to write that down, and save it," she sputtered. "I've maybe been overly critical lately."

We returned just before lunch. "How was your ride?" Erin asked, with a warm smile.

"Great!" I replied.

Bill's girlfriend, who lived in town, was helping Erin fix sandwiches and soup. We all sat down at the table: the young French boy, quiet and attentive; Erin and Heather; their husbands; and the two small boys. Bill sat at the head of the table. His personality dominated the room. It was easy to see why Erin was building a house beyond sight of the ranch, to have a home life that felt like hers.

After lunch I relaxed on the front porch, dawdling, while everyone returned to their chores. And there was plenty to go around. Erin worked full time with Bill at the ranch, while everybody else had weekday jobs. Weekends, they all pitched in. And frankly, I didn't know how they did it. The responsibility was everything Connie and I had plus cattle ranching, horseback riding, and serving two more guest meals a day!

The family dynamics were fascinating to watch, as Heather tried to please Bill, Erin attempted to raise two boys while managing everything else, and Bill relegated himself to family patriarch, meaning well, while never filtering a word he said. The two husbands spent time horseshoeing, haying, and generally staying in good spirits by keeping out of everybody's else's way.

Later that evening I wandered down to the living room and pulled out a photo album on display. A light was on in the kitchen. I sat down at the table by the window. It was dark outside, and I heard some thunder rumble.

"That'll bring the horses back to the corral," Bill said, appearing out of his room. "Mind if I join you?"

"Please do," I said.

"Care for a beer?" Bill asked, handing me a bottle while refilling his glass with scotch, before sitting next to me at the table. "Those are photos of my guiding days," he said, glancing at the album.

The pages were a compendium of his life, with pictures going back years of Bill posing next to hunters with their game.

"I was President of the Wildlife Conservation Society for years," Bill said. "Mountain sheep have a lifespan of twelve years, and we never shot a young one. People don't understand that regulated hunting maintains a necessary balance."

"How did you get back into these places?" I asked, noticing several locales in the middle of frozen wilderness.

"I was a bush pilot, sometimes that got us up to the camps. Other times, if need be, we'd go by packhorse," he said. "It won't be long before nobody knows how to rig a packhorse. It's a skill that's disappearing. Do it wrong and it all ends up in the river."

Bill took a sip from his glass. "I had a guy die on me once out there. Had to bend him over a fallen tree before rigamortis set in, so I could come back with my horse and haul him out."

Cowboys like to shock you. They like to say things like this, calmly, as though it's part of everyday conversation. Your job is not to flinch, as though this is part of your own experience, and you naturally understand, without betraying your true thoughts, "ARE YOU FUCKING KIDDING ME!"

I had little time for a retort. The best I could come up with was, "You probably knew he wasn't going to make it. I reckon you could have told him to kindly fold himself over a log before drawing his last breath."

I looked deep into Bill's eyes. He didn't flinch. Nothing betrayed what I knew he was thinking, "ARE YOU FUCKING KIDDING ME!" He just poured another drink. "Yup, I reckon you're right."

I asked him about his girlfriend. He didn't really want to talk about her. He wanted to talk about his wife. A picture of her looking healthy and happy hung on the wall by the door. "I never thought she'd go before me." His eyes suddenly looked sad. "I'd give anything for it to be the other way around."

The next morning at breakfast Bill said he was riding up into the hills to fetch a bull with an infected hoof so he could bring it down to the back corral and fill the bull up with penicillin for a week. The French boy and his girlfriend were going. Did I want to come along?

"Sure," I replied, sensing a unique adventure.

Still covered in dew, the foliage had a sweet aroma as we set off beyond the hills. Bill's wiry dog charged ahead, returning repeatedly to the horses' heels, energized she had something useful to do.

"The first thing we have to do is find the bull," Bill said. We passed several small bunches of cattle, as Bill stretched in his saddle, peering further ahead into the hills

Bill led us across a rushing stream. "After a good thunderstorm I'll sometimes find buffalo skulls jutting out from the creek beds. Relics from the old Indian days."

We rode for more than an hour before Bill pointed to a clump of trees. "There he is."

Bill trotted up, circled behind the trees, and began shouting cowboy yelps while the dog ran in, barking wildly, and flushed the bull out into the open. The bull must have weighed two thousand pounds. It was huge. And with a painful infection, it wasn't to be trifled with.

"Give me room," Bill hollered, and he lassoed a rope round the bull's thick neck.

"Okay, I've got him," Bill said. He positioned his horse a few yards behind the bull, and shouted the bull forward down a grassy incline. Bill's girlfriend, the French boy, and I followed a short distance behind. Suddenly, with no warning, the bull bellowed, stood on its hind legs, twisted in a violent spasm and planted its front hooves on the flank of Bill's panicked horse.

Bill's horse reared up. His girlfriend whirled her horse around to the right, as did I, followed by the French boy. I turned around. Bill's horse was part way down the hill. The bull stood heaving its massive chest, angry, still lassoed to the rope. And on the other end of the rope, twenty yards away, on his knees, his eyes locked on the bull, was Bill.

In an instant this had suddenly turned into a life or death situation. The bull could charge any minute. Bill was defenseless. And there wasn't a damn thing we could do about it! A sudden move could precipitate a charge.

"Get me my horse," Bill said to his girlfriend, quietly, remaining perfectly still. She sat on her horse, frozen, staring at the bull.

"Get me my horse *now*. Can you not see that I'm in a predicament?"

She slowly dismounted, held on to her reins, and walked watchfully over to Bill's horse, and nervously brought the horse up beside him. He climbed back on, steadied himself, and we headed back down the trail, this time keeping the bull at a safer distance.

———•———

The next day, cooled by a nice breeze, I sat on the verandah, feeling like I'd learned a little more about ranching. None of these people would be easy to forget. They'd all gone about their lives, treating me with kindness, and in one way or another made me feel as though I belonged. However brief the moments may have been, I felt we had shared a special connection. I hated to leave. It felt like I'd just gotten to know them.

One-by-one the next morning I said goodbye to Erin and Heather and Bill. And insisted, if they are anywhere near Banff, I'd love to have them visit.

Chapter 21

No longer an 'and' . . .
but an 'or'

"Ping." What's that?

"Ping . . . ping." No way.

"PingPingPingPingPing . . . I can't believe it! That's hail. We're in the middle of a hail storm."

"Paddle," I shouted. "It's freezing!"

Connie laughed, "Next time I'll bring a helmet!"

Only in Banff, in August, perspiring from one of the summer's hottest days, dressed only in shorts and t-shirts, could you be canoeing on Vermillion Lakes, and suddenly find yourself under a dark cloud being pelted by hail stones . . . with nowhere near to hide.

We finally paddled under a tree and waited out the storm, amazed by the ice pellets now refrigerating the floor of the canoe. Thirty minutes later, wet and shivering, sitting in the car with the heat on, Connie glanced up and grinned, "Welcome to Banff, home of the slogan, 'Eat dessert first, life's unpredictable!'"

—·—

Banff has two local newspapers, the old and venerable, *Crag and Canyon,* and the comparative upstart, the better designed, more reader friendly *Rocky Mountain Outlook*. For decades the *Crag and Canyon* enjoyed a monopoly. It's founder, Norman Luxton, a handsome entrepreneur, had had his hand in just about everything, including a popular trading post that was the center of commerce for the tourists, the locals, and the Stoney Indians. As a writer himself, and author of a travelogue autobiography, it wasn't a stretch for Luxton to usher in the first local newspaper.

As Bow Valley prospered so too did the *Crag and Canyon,* earning revenues, like most newspapers, from local advertisers and healthy subscription fees. But all that changed a decade ago when a plucky editor, Carol Picard, decided that if Bow Valley could support one paper, then why not two. Working eighty hour weeks on a shoestring budget she launched the *Outlook*, and to the consternation of the *Crag and Canyon*, she distributed it to the local residents for free.

Nothing devours cash faster than a print publication, but the *Outlook* held on, ultimately forcing the *Crag and Canyon* to drop their subscription fees. And today, unlike the contraction and demise of many big city papers, both local papers are thriving.

Why? Because everybody reads them. But more importantly because small town papers have an advantage big city paper's don't: for their advertisers there's nowhere else to go—no metropolitan magazines, radio or TV stations competing for their advertising dollar. This is it.

One paper comes out on Tuesdays and the other paper appears on Thursdays, and fortunately for all involved, the townsfolk have a peculiar enjoyment reading what is often the exact same news twice. For those who might sneer at this small town mentality, I say, "Not so fast, buffalo breath!" The news is indeed limited . . . but fascinating. Imagine reading, "Irate elk puts hoof through bakery window," below the headline, "French baker quits in a huff!" Twice? You bet, I can't wait to see a competing reporter's take on this one!

But here's what's different today about living in a small town, and it's changed fairly recently. Today, you can have the best of both worlds, all the benefits of small town life while being as intellectually stimulated by global events as you want to be. I subscribe to the *National Post,* Canada's conservative national paper (as opposed to reading the liberal *Globe and Mail,* which quickly bores me because I agree with most of its views), and thanks to cable TV I watch "Meet the Press," and "This Week," on Sunday mornings, just like I always have. And these examples don't touch on the access to news and events—tabloid suffused they may be—available today on the internet. This is a new phenomenon. The choice of a simpler way of life, *and* the stimulation that comes from being connected to a global world, is now an "and" . . . not an "or."

But just as modern-day communications has eliminated the feelings of small town isolation, it's an illusion to think that tentacles from afar can't reach out and darkly touch us . . . leaving us nearly nowhere to hide.

I was riveted by the business news of the last few years, in shock like nearly everyone else, while trying to measure the seismic impact. First Bear Stearns, then Lehman Brothers, followed by Merrill Lynch, Citibank, and others, had all gone belly up. Wall Street and America had essentially gone bankrupt. And it had all unraveled in a matter of weeks. A perfect storm of greed, stupidity, and negligence had driven the western world to the brink of financial collapse.

The stock market had gyrated downwards at mind boggling speed while the U.S. Federal Reserve pumped hundreds of billions into the banking system to try to restore liquidity (which is a banking euphemism for, "We're busted. Flat out broke. Ain't nothin but a hobo now. You're going to have to print some money and give it to us idiots real fast!").

Canadian banks, though, were sound due to tighter oversight and regulations. And suddenly these rule abiding "Don't Walk" adherents didn't look so silly. ("Hey, Gringo. How's that jay walking working out? You no see that big truck, señor?" Canadians have a history of wintering in Mexico. Some of them actually talk like this.) But when the United States sneezes, Canada catches a cold. And the United States had come down with typhoid fever.

Since tourists' travel plans and reservations are often made long in advance Connie reasoned that there would be a delayed affect. It would take time before Banff ran into the headwinds. The larger, more expensive hotels and restaurants would feel it first, followed eventually by everyone else. "Fortunately, the B&B has only three rooms to fill," Connie said, "which might give us a little protection."

In the meantime the central banks in both the United States and Canada (in Canada's case, to protect its currency) had been slashing interest rates, bailing out the banks on the backs of retirees and savers. In the ensuing months interest rates had been cut three times.

As we watched the unfolding debacle I only prayed there was a silver lining somewhere in all of this, but if there was, at the present moment, we sure couldn't see it.

Chapter 22

Rattled

The ideal woman? What does a man want? Assuming he thought about it, these three items might top the list. Someone to whom he is physically attracted. A woman who is intellectually stimulating; not to be confused with knowledge, curiosity will do. And a woman who generates tender emotions, periodically, enjoyed most often in his eagerness to protect her. Three out of three, very hard to find, and when we do it's the closest we ever come to love. True love!

What does a woman desire? I'm just guessing, but it could be intelligence, empathy, and fortitude. Not easy to find. Almost impossible. Practically a futile effort. But when they do, here's what they feel. Ardor. Romantic ardor. And that's exactly what men want! We say we want love. We don't. Love means staying put, dirty dishes, stinky diapers. Bad. Bad. Bad. Ardor means sex, cooked meals and forgiveness. Good. Good. Good. Ask any of them, Marc Antony, Don Juan, Mohatma Ghandi. Love versus ardor? Ardor every time!

But here's the thing. Ardor comes and goes. And when it goes it doesn't fade or wane, it suddenly evaporates. Poof. Gone.

And then we have to get it back. Not easy . . . but possible . . . if the winds of luck are blowing in our direction.

———————

I woke up rattled. Fearful. Over what, I had no idea. When you're young fear is identifiable, attached to something specific. Dad's going to go ape shit when he discovers I broke his car window. Spike promised to beat me up after school. The algebra test . . . I'm going to fail it, because I have no idea what the teacher's been talking about. How could I? I've been dreaming about Rebecca in the front row, dutifully taking her notes.

And they all come true! Dad did go ape shit. Spike delivered on his promise. I did get an F while Rebecca got an A. Anyway, as thousands of similar calamities accumulate over a lifetime, by middle age, fear doesn't need a reason. Sumpin's gonna happen. I don't know what it is. But sumpin. And I was right.

The afternoon was perfect, hotter than usual, but lovely. Connie and I hadn't meant to go on a hike, just a drive, but as we drove near the trail to Spray Loop we couldn't resist. "We'll just go a mile and turn back," I said. We hadn't brought any water, but then again we weren't going to go that far.

The trail meandered through the woods and along the river. A breeze tempered the heat of the sun. We walked for thirty minutes. "Should we turn back?" I asked.

"We've barely started," Connie replied. I felt toastily refreshed as well. We kept going. A sign up ahead appeared. "Three kilometers to the end."

"We've already hiked two miles. Only a ways to go," I pronounced. "Why not?"

By the time we arrived at the turnaround the sun had risen high above us, and any trace of a breeze had ended. We sat on a log by a wooden bridge, happy to be there, mopping the perspiration from our foreheads. And then we hiked back. Hot, sweaty, and tired.

The house was empty of guests. That evening Connie made a nice fish dinner, and we retired to bed early, exhausted. In the middle of the night I awoke to painful cramps. It felt like someone was throwing javelins in my lower abdomen. I staggered up and walked across the floor to the bathroom. Whatever it was got worse. In addition to the stabs of pain, cold, clammy shivers started to sweep through my flesh in waves. And then it seemed to subside. I'd just have to sleep through it. I stood and began to walk back to the bedroom. Something was immediately wrong. The room began spinning. My legs buckled underneath me. I felt the sharp corner of a table and everything started to go black. "Connie!" I hollered out, and then I collapsed unconscious on a chair.

As though time had been suspended I suddenly felt my arms and legs thrusting out, trying to awaken my senses. I felt Connie holding me. I could hear her panicked voice, muffled, shouting into the phone. "Yes, I'll place him on the floor! When will the ambulance get here? Please hurry!"

And then slowly she and the room came into view. Someone knocked on the door, and three men in uniforms burst into the house. One knelt beside me. Another grabbed my wrist. "Was I a diabetic? Did I have heart problems?" Someone pricked my finger. "His glucose is fine."

Connie was still frantic, describing how she found me, as one of the rescue workers tried to calm her down. "All your vital signs are fine," said one of the men. "Do you think you can walk?"

"I don't think so," I said, having no idea why I was lying there in the first place. They brought in a stretcher, hoisted me up and carried me out to the ambulance. It was three A.M. By the time we got to the hospital, and they hooked me up to fluids in the emergency room, I began to feel stronger. I didn't have my contacts in. Everything was in a blur, like an impressionist painting. (I'm convinced if Monet had been handed a pair of glasses he'd have looked at his work and said, "What the fuck is that?").

The doctor approached. He'd been talking to the rescue team. I braced myself. A brain tumor? The big C? I had to be strong for Connie. Through withered eyes I looked up at Connie. And what did I see? Believe it or not, ardor. My impending demise had somehow produced romantic ardor.

"What happened Doc?"

"You fainted."

"I what?"

"You fainted."

Connie's jaw dropped open. She looked at her watch. Did I mention that ardor is a fickle thing?

"Yup, looks like you fainted. Did you not drink any water all day? We've already put two bags of fluid into you."

I told him about our hike. He nodded and went on to explain. "You were dehydrated from the heat, the salty fish didn't help, and whatever you ate disagreed with you. Blood rushes to the site of the pain, and all that causes your blood pressure to drop, which combined, caused you to faint."

"But I drank plenty of water when I returned from the hike," I said.

"Water isn't enough. It doesn't replace the minerals you lose when you're perspiring heavily. You need electrolytes. I suggest that you purchase a box called Gastrolytes. They're available over the counter. The box has packets of powder containing minerals that you can dissolve into water. I never go on long treks in the Rockies without them."

I bounced back in a couple of days, and continued to caution our guests to carry plenty of fluids when hiking in the Canadian Rockies, while adding at times for emphasis, "I know from whence I speak."

———•———

Pleasure can be found in the simplest accomplishments, and little compared in this moment to the look and smell of fresh cut grass. I plunked down on the lawn in a shady spot, a short distance from where I'd silenced the mower. The days had rolled on, seemingly sheltered by the encircling mountains, but as the financial carnage spread out from the states, causing hardship for millions, Canada's economy was still willfully brisk, and interest in Connie's house had suddenly picked up considerably.

Connie pretended not to notice, but the real estate agent had shown the house twice to one couple, and indicated that two other prospects were anxious to see the home. Someone was bound to make an offer, and if it was reasonable Connie would have little choice. But I wasn't convinced that selling the B&B, a home she loved, was her only option. The policies being driven by the U.S. economic disaster had given me an idea. Maybe, just maybe, the winds of luck were blowing in her direction.

Connie noticed me sitting on the grass and came and sat beside me. Tall sunflowers she had planted earlier, now fragile, had begun to break at their stem. "Connie, can I ask you something? I know the B&B is a lot of work, but if you didn't have to sell the house would you sell it?"

She sat still, before slowly shaking her head no.

"Well, maybe you don't have to."

"Yes, I do," she said. "It's in our agreement." Her eyes looked down. "First the marriage falls apart, and it wasn't even my fault, and now this."

"What if you bought him out?"

"With what? How could I do that?"

"The down payment you put on the house was yours. His share of the equity isn't little, but it isn't huge. Due to the financial mess, banks have been dropping interest rates considerably, over two percentage points since you put the house on the market. I'll bet you could refinance the loan, including his payout, at these lower rates without changing your payments that much?"

"Do you think?"

"It's worth finding out."

The next morning Connie's mortgage broker called back with the new numbers. Connie found me in the back yard. "At these new lower interest rates I can put it all in my name and the payments will increase by less than a hundred dollars a month!"

"That's terrific! Let's celebrate."

"We are," Connie said, and grinning, she held up the For Sale sign she'd already removed from the window.

———.———

The next morning I wandered out to the back deck with a cup of coffee, and gazed out at Connie's garden and the red painted fence. How ironic, I thought, that Canada's economy has always been linked to America's prosperity, yet Connie's B&B was inadvertently rescued by America's financial calamity.

Chapter 23
What's in a name?

They start it, and then I get in trouble . . . unless, of course, it's a Brit! I knew I was in for fun when Mike and Glynis arrived from England. We get visitors from around the globe, but the Brits outnumber the other nationalities by far.

Canada is part of the British Commonwealth, and from what I'd observed, Canadians are as proud of their British heritage as they are of their independence. There isn't a single holiday celebrating a Canadian, but Victoria Day reigns supreme every May!

I love the Brits' sense of decorum, and their ability to converse about anything, but most of all I savor their wry, dry wit. Over breakfast one morning, a Manchester father discussing his teenage son, said, "I told him there's nothing anymore I can do to him. The only thing left is to crucify him on the garage door."

And now Mike and Glynis had arrived. After reading Connie's small sign inside the front door, "Thank you for removing your shoes at the door. Your thoughtful consideration is appreciated!" Mike balanced himself precariously, refusing to move, his toes on the edge of the entry rug, as though the hardwood floor was at the bottom of the Grand Canyon.

They had arrived in Banff via Cleveland where they'd attended a family reunion, an enclave of British descendants drawn to jobs in America's rust belt of iron and steel mills. "I couldn't believe how many cousins we had," Mike said. "And how they welcomed us with such enthusiasm!"

"You're their contemporary ancestors," I said. "Their missing link. Jane Goodall would be proud!"

The next day after a personalized tour of the two fireplaces, Mike asked, "Is Jamie short for James?"

"No, it's my given name."

"It's got to be short for something," he teased. "I think I'll call you Jim. It's so American!"

"I prefer Bwana, it sort of rolls off your tongue."

Well, one thing led to another, and on his departure I slipped this little epistle onto his car windshield:

I think we should go into a partnership . . .
the possibilities are mind boggling!

Fearless Mike
And
Bwana Jim's
(notice how I gave you top billing)
Honeymoon Safari Tour

- Learn the mating call of the Canadian moose—it will help you and the moose when hiking alone in the Northwest Territories.

- Experience first-hand the lusty habits of elk, bear and mountain sheep . . . ram will have a whole new meaning! (Purchase this educational video, narrated by Fearless Mike—fun for the whole family!)

- Don't forget the internationally famous Fireplace Tour—25 cents—by Bwana Jim.

- Learn how generations of inbreeding have made Fearless Mike an expert on wildlife!

- Discover priceless trivia, like why Canada replaced the Union Jack with a marijuana leaf . . . to the delight of Prince Charles and Camilla, and what country in its right mind has a beaver as its symbol?

All this, and much more—cash in advance please!

Connie and I were out doing errands when Mike and Glynis departed the B&B, along with my tender missive. I knew there was no way I wouldn't hear from Mike again, a clever retort, a thrust and parry, sumpin! The following arrived by email the next evening:

Dear Connie and Bwana Jim:

You are not going to believe what happened to us last night at 9:15 pm at Moraine Lake Lodge. Glynis and I found ourselves within thirty meters of a mother grizzly bear and her two cubs!!

Don't worry, Fearless Mike and Glynis, without pepper spray (I'd left it in our room) coped admirably. We calmly remained seated and continued to eat our evening meal whilst we watched the three bears from the dining room!!

Thanks for everything!

All the best, Mike and Glynis

———•———

No sooner did Mike and Glynis check out than Jane and Will checked in. Jane and Will weren't their real names. From the Orient, they had given themselves American names while traveling abroad to Canada. For our future trip to China, Connie and I didn't know many Asian names to choose from. Thankfully, with Jane's and Will's help we will now be traveling proudly as Maling and Ziaoping.

———•———

Connie and I made an executive decision, a courageous decision, little different from those companies that years ago announced they were "smoke free." We decided to cancel our Wifi connection. From now on for guests who ask for our Wifi pass code we will politely reply, "I am sorry, we don't have Wifi."

It hit a tipping point when two days in a row a laptop appeared at the breakfast table, and moments later a guest complained in a panic that the signal was not strong enough for his smart phone. And the week prior, as I was explaining the B&B to a couple, the newly arrived husband was instead fixated on his tablet, trying to get online.

"What's happening to my B&B?" Connie exclaimed. "We are turning into an internet café, with guests sitting in the living room on their computers instead of conversing with one another, forcing us and the other guests to tiptoe around them quietly." Connie was right. Quickly disappearing was the Gatsby era experience we cherished for us and our guests. Modern technology, like smoking, had created a solution for a problem that never existed. For decades people had enjoyed the Canadian Rockies, and each other, without the need to be transported to another world.

We both knew this decision was risky, an uphill fight against a cultural phenomenon, sure to spark a few complaints, but I admired Connie for her altruistic stance. "At a time when human connectivity is more important than ever," she said, "I can at least try to preserve it at my tiny B&B."

"So how's that working out for you?" an internet sociologist might ask.

"Well, interesting." From the moment we told our first guests that we didn't have a Wifi connection, for Connie and I it was sheer bliss. Almost instantly the B&B returned to its recent past. Couples began talking to each other. Guests began conversing with one another. A tranquil, unhurried mood settled upon us like snowflakes drifting aimlessly to the ground.

A friend who took guests on overnight sailing trips had also complained vociferously, "After dinner we used to all sit outside under the stars and talk. Now everyone takes out their tablets. They're on them all day!" We felt vindicated, part of a shrinking minority, but at least not alone. And for the first few weeks, when told there was no internet service, the guests merely shrugged, unfazed.

But we had been warned. Told of our plans to cancel the service, Connie's brother-in-law looked up from his smart phone, and sputtered, "Ohhhhhh, I wouldn't do that." So a part of us waited in trepidation . . . and neither of us was fully prepared.

Howard and Nicky, a couple in their thirties from New York, checked in. I introduced them to the B&B, and then took them out back where I spread out my maps, and told them about day trips and scenic hikes in the area. They were happy. Their stay would be short. Tonight and the next day, and then they were off. And then Nicky asked if we had Wifi.

"No, I'm sorry, we don't," I replied.

"What do you mean you don't?"

"I'm afraid you're out of luck," I said, trying to lighten the moment. Big mistake. Nicky wasn't used to being told she was out of luck . . . about anything.

"What do you mean I'm out of luck?" Nicky stammered.

Feeling alarmed, though their time off the internet would only be one day, I relayed that we'd had the service, but cancelled it, and politely explained the reasons why. Bigger mistake. I could read Nicky's thoughts. Who was I to pass such judgments? This wasn't about the internet. To Nicky, it was about her.

Their final morning I knew we were in trouble when Nicky and Howard came to breakfast, and avoided our friendly glances. They were steamed. Having found their way online, they had done some research and, misguided, had followed their GPS up Corey Pass, a strenuous, treacherous incline.

Perhaps their misadventure contributed to their malaise, for when Howard checked out he angrily confronted Connie. They'd apparently gone out and purchased a seventy dollar gadget the night before to link themselves up to the internet. Taken aback, Connie took seventy dollars off their two-night bill.

Connie and I looked at each other. Well, that didn't go very well. Surely, we could learn something from this. And we did.

A week later another couple checked in for two nights. He was a computer scientist—a curious fellow, wearing ear muffs in the summer heat. He had a serious demeanor, and seemed to take social cues from others. So Connie and I smiled a lot.

"Do you have Wifi?" he asked, after I'd shown them the maps.

"No, I'm sorry, we don't," I replied. I offered no explanation. I sensed some mild discomfort. "If it's important to you, we're just a small B&B, but the hotels across the street have it, and we won't charge you if you'd prefer to stay elsewhere."

He looked at his wife. They quietly conferred. "Thank you," he said, "for the offer. We are happy to stay here."

It was perfect. They might have been disappointed, but it wasn't directed at us. We'd adjusted some valves, tinkered with our communications, and solved our problem. Almost. Six days later Connie collared me downstairs, and implored, "Please come up and explain the B&B to the new arrivees. He's already got his tablet out, and they're staying for seven nights. I can't refill a whole week!"

He said he worked in technology. This wasn't going to be easy. Connie and I instinctively plied them with treats. She brought out tea. Then she laid out a crumb cake and biscuits. I went over the maps, giving them all the local tips I could muster, while Connie offered the coup de grace, the use of our washing machine and dryer if needed, all in hopes of mitigating the dreaded question, which finally came, "Do you have Wifi?"

I poured his tea. "I'm sorry we don't."

His wife seemed unbothered. But a strange sound began emitting from his throat, something inhuman, somewhere between a wheeze and a choke.

Connie could hear it from the kitchen. Calmly, she walked out, not knowing the cause, and politely handed him a glass of water . . . this is clearly a work in progress.

*Note to readers: Wifi stands for wireless internet access. By the time this is published it may not exist. Many may have lined up for frontal lobe implants linked directly to some kind of hologram visible to cyber space at all times.

On a sobering note, we are beginning to see that our obsession with all things digital, while neglecting the old-fashioned book, has consequences. CBS reported recently that the U.S. SAT scores for college bound students were in, and it showed that 57% of the tested were not ready for college. Reading scores were the worst in forty years!

**Connie and I finally caved. We now give out our Wifi password freely, and we're okay with it . . . really, we are.

Chapter 24
. . . back by Christmas

I noticed red buffalo berries had suddenly appeared on the green bushes. Thousands of them brightened the sides of the trails where the sun was the most abundant. The bears had begun fattening up on them for their winter hibernation. The nights had begun to turn cool. And it wouldn't be long before the elk and the deer and the mountain sheep thickened their brown coats. Summer was coming to an end.

When someone dies unexpectedly, before their time, they often linger in your thoughts, returning from time to time, far more frequently than if they were still alive. Throughout our days we often search for some pattern to our existence, perhaps making more of our choices and life's coincidences, to take comfort in a belief that there is some invisible hand helping to guide our destiny.

And then a death occurs to someone we know, someone we liked, someone irreplaceable in multiple ways, and the randomness of it all leaves us stunned. And that's how I felt now.

A news clipping in the *Calgary Herald* had filtered up from the Skyline Ranch, my temporary sanctuary in the Porcupine Hills. Erin, Bill's daughter, the former rodeo queen, and mother of two small boys, had been killed when a three-wheeled vehicle she was riding overturned, perhaps thrown by a rock or culvert hidden by the tall, green grass.

And if Bill, still grieving from the loss of his wife, was the soul of this B&B and ranch, Erin had been very much its heart.

The pain of loss, I've noticed, seems to target different parts of the body. There's the loss as you grow older of activities you once did, things you felt passionate about, that for some reason no longer interest you. Something triggers the memory—a couple sailing, perhaps a photo of someone backpacking through exotic locales—and there's a tinge of sadness, a part of you seems to have come and gone. But the nostalgia is often confined to your head, mitigated by the awareness you don't *want* to do those things anymore . . . new pleasures have comfortably taken their place.

And then there's the loss of a companion: a friend, a loved one, a family pet. And the heart really does take the brunt of the pain, sharp stabs followed by a hollowed out sense of emptiness, until eventually all the anger and confusion fall back from their heightened state.

I'd lived long enough to say goodbye to a few former selves, and a philosophy of, "It's better to have loved and lost than to never have loved at all," has produced equal measures of joy and pain. But until now I'd never experienced the pain from a loss of place. Not really. And as I prepared to leave Banff, as I wandered by familiar places—the bicycle rim hidden in the tree, the Bow River rippling gently along, the mists drifting among the mountain peaks, even the U-back Café—I felt a despair in my chest, a weight that sunk to the bottom of my stomach.

As I heaved my suitcase into the trunk—my heart, my head, and my chest all aching—I told Connie, "I'll be back by Christmas. The time will go fast. I promise."

"No it won't. It will seem like forever," she said, choking back tears.

I slowly backed out of the driveway. A few blocks up Banff Avenue a young man hesitated by the side of the road, and the car in front of me politely stopped, as did I and the cars behind me, waiting patiently for him to cross. Then I drove past the "Welcome to Banff" sign with Bill Peyto's striking visage, and turned east onto the Trans-Canada highway.

———·———

I decided to take the meandering way to the Montana border, through Kananaskis and along the Cowboy Trail, clinging to views of the Rockies as long as possible. Three hours later I passed the gravel road turn-off to Bill's ranch, fighting the urge to connect in some meaningful way, knowing it was all too soon.

The autumn colors brightened the further I drove south. The highway wound back into the Rockies, past the picturesque village inside Waterton Lakes, over the border, and into Glacier National Park. National parks, provincial parks, state parks, and city parks; I marveled at those who had the wisdom to designate and preserve them, while not envying the task of managing them.

Managing natural resources, I'd come to understand, is no easy matter. Just as developers are pitted against preservationists inside a tourist town, outside it's a constant balancing act, with park personnel serving a mandate to meet the needs of sportsmen, recreationists, environmentalists, and commercial concerns. And the hunter, the snowmobiler, the logger, and the protector of the white spotted owl, are not always moved by the other's interests. For the superintendants, every decision leaves somebody perturbed.

Banff National Park, enlarged by adjacent parks Yoho, Jasper, Kootenay and Kananaskis*, was Canada's first national park, the very first tract of wilderness set aside in 1887 by the government for permanent protection.** But the creation of duly designated parks actually began in the fifteenth century, with a decided mix of noble intent and confusion, little different from what some might believe continues to persist today.

Well, maybe the intent wasn't so noble, at least not in the fifteenth century when aristocratic Europeans set aside hunting preserves exclusively for their own use. Then in the seventeenth and eighteenth centuries somewhat prissier noblemen hired landscape architects to create vast topiary gardens with walkways and flowers and a few ornamental deer and cows grazing, for the express pleasure of . . . themselves.

Cities, however, gradually expanded, encroaching on these opulent grounds until public demands by city dwellers for an escape from city life made parks such as New York's Central Park a customary piece of city planning. At the same time amusement parks, accompanied by carousels, and restaurants, and romantic lagoons, began springing up in Europe and the U.S., often located at the end of rail spurs, sparked by railroad companies to generate passengers.

But it was America's national parks, first Yosemite in 1864 followed by Yellowstone in 1872, with their geysers, waterfalls, and majestic peaks, that were preserved for travelers to stand in awe of

* The park was named after an Indian who survived an axe rebuke to his head. Kananaskis was his name, though he never could pronounce it very well after that!

This is a good place to bring up the name "Indian." A Stoney elder announced, "I'm an Indian, not a Native American, nor a First Nation's person. Those are just names that the white man calls us to assuage their guilt."

** This was all the more admirable considering at the time the threat wasn't as obvious. The Western population was sparse, uncrowded and uncongested. The adjacent town of Canmore had less than 500 residents compared to more than 17,000 today.

their natural beauty, just as voyagers to Europe stood in awe of the Parthenon, Rome's Coliseum, and the ruins of ancient cities. And it wasn't unusual for medicinal purposes to designate newly discovered hot springs, often surrounded by picturesque settings, as protected reserves, reminiscent of the Roman and Turkish baths of antiquity, no different from the origins of Banff National Park. Yet over time there is little in Banff National Park's history that hasn't touched on the narrative of most parks, from an early focus as a playground for the rich to the restorative powers of a spa to the eclectic mish mash of an amusement park.

In fact in the 1950s, with the importation of buffalo and elk for the tourists and the culling of dangerous predators such as the wolf and the cougar, not to mention the addition of a golf course, wax museum, pavilions for band concerts, and even a zoo (tourists could be seen feeding bears from the side of the road . . . always fun for the locals on hiking trails), Banff's original, alluring identity as the mountaineering "Switzerland of Canada" had begun to mingle with the scruffy ideals of Coney Island. And for the first thirty years, all of this merged commercially with loggers hauling timber, and smoke billowing from a coal mining tipple barely five miles outside town.

But little known to historians, the manipulation of wildlife for the benefit of the tourists created Canada's first welfare recipient . . . the beaver. Not originally indigenous to the Rockies, a forest fire in 1904 destroyed acres of spruce and fir trees while leaving groves of poplar to become embedded along the rivers, and the beavers migrated westward from the foothills to this last remaining food source.

Beaver ponds multiplied, tourists were entertained, and everyone was happy . . . except for the Medical Officer of Health who in the late 1940s feared these furry rodents were contaminating Banff's unfiltered water. The beaver was suddenly banished along with their favorite tree. But Elvis had not left the building . . . not by a long shot. The beaver had become popular, and as their population grew scarce, and tourists complained, Special Warden Hubert U. Green bowed to the pressure, which led to the planting of several poplars west of Vermillion Lakes where an artificially fed beaver could sunbathe, swim, and amuse himself to no end, to the tourists' delight. And I have little doubt that this one happy beaver deserves much of the credit for the Park's common vision today that its unspoiled wilderness and wildlife takes precedence over most other concerns.

———

I drove peacefully along, traversing the country, before dumping myself for a day of rest in Grand Rapids, Minnesota. What to do? What anyone would do. Learn how to saw a huge log in half. I visited the Grand Rapids Forest History Center where a replica of a turn-of-the-century logging camp had been erected. Locals, dressed in period costumes portraying lumberjacks, saw filers, cooks, and clerks, gave a riveting demonstration of life in the backwoods. Cold, dangerous, and isolated. The camps were inhabited by immigrants who worked all winter in order to supplement their farming income.

The term, "You have to know when to push and when to pull" didn't originate, I discovered, among lumberjacks. Trying my skills at a two-handed six-foot saw, a fellow tourist and I were told, "Never push. Get into a rhythm where each only pulls. You don't damage the blade, and it's a hell of a lot easier!"

But Grand Rapids was home to another attraction. Brochures and signs proudly announced that the town was the birthplace of Judy Garland. Sure enough, her childhood home, a cuddly white house on the edge of town, had been converted into a museum, where each summer the front yard is ablaze with poppies, just like the field in the *Wizard of Oz*.

But unfortunately, at the age of four, Judy and her family moved to California. A photo at a nearby exhibit showed a 1949 high school graduating class. "The kids Judy would have known had she stayed," read the caption. It was sad, all the way around. You could see it in the eyes of the high school graduates.

Leaving Minnesota, I veered off the main highway in search of a country road. Past a century old general store, along a winding road, a billboard suddenly appeared. (Billboards do that in the States.) It read something like this. "Adults only campground!" Interesting, I thought. "Nude camping." More interesting, I reflected. "Sex games and activities." Well now, what's this all about? And then I got to the bottom line. "Bikers welcome!" It didn't say, "Former cheerleaders welcome," nor "Ex-bunnies welcome." It said, "Bikers welcome!"

They say that the best writing triggers the imagination. Indeed it did . . . and none of it included getting out of there alive! Quickly moving on, cured of my prurient interest, I vowed that my image of farm fresh Minnesota would remain resolute.

Three days later I arrived home in northern Virginia, a suburb of Washington D.C. It was rainy and windy the next morning when I drove out for groceries. It was a four-lane road lined with strip malls, gas stations, and fast food restaurants. A pregnant woman stood in the middle of the road holding the hand of a small child.

She was not at a light or a crosswalk, but she was there. And she needed to get her pregnant self and little boy across. I stopped. Cars behind me honked angrily. Cars in the right lane kept whizzing by. Finally, other drivers took notice, and allowed her to scurry across.

Home sweet home.

Chapter 25
"Didn't see that coming . . ."

If I were teaching a grade school civics class I'd have to say, "Children, what follows is a tale of Shakesperean dimensions, a tale of tragedy, comedy, betrayal, abdication, and subterfuge."

"Mr. MacVicar, the children are only six years old."

"Please, I am trying to teach a class. You've all heard the expression, *possession is nine tenths of the law*, and nobody knows that better than you. Well, kids, that's true. Unless what you possess is shit, I mean real *shit*, yours and everybody else's, and then it's nine tenths *your* problem. May I start from the beginning?"

The phone rings. I'm in Virginia. It's Connie. "I'm standing in shit!"

"What?"

"I'm standing in muck. Raw sewage. The pipe has backed up and flooded the basement cement floor."

I stifled the urge to joke, "Now aren't you glad you bought the house?"

"What do I do?"

I knew she'd asked a rhetorical question. "Call a plumber."

"I just did. The problem is this just happened a little over a year ago! And it cost me over seven hundred dollars to auger out the pipe."

"Then in that case you'd better have them take a camera and see what's causing the blockage, and more importantly, is the clog happening on your property or town property. If it's town property than Banff will have to pay for it."

The next day Connie phoned again. "Great news! Bernard, the plumber, routed out the pipe and unplugged the mess. Tree roots had worked their way in. Then he snaked in his camera. The clog was several meters from our property, on town property approaching the main line."

"Fantastic," I said. "I'll call Bernard myself, and see where we go from here. What was the cost?"

"It was almost $750."

I called the plumber. "Bernard, Connie tells me you found the source of the problem."

"Yup, sure did. Those pipes are decades old, and roots crawl in at the cracks, and cause the back up."

"Well, at least the blockage is clearly on town property. How do we pass the costs on to them?"

"Well, therein lies a problem. The town passed a bylaw last year that says the property owner is now responsible all the way to the main line in the middle of the street."

"You've got to be kidding me! Were any property owners present?"

Bernard snickered quietly. You see Bernard was in a bit of a pickle. He insinuated by his tone that the homeowners were getting shafted, but he also did plumbing work for the town. "Half the homes in Banff are impacted by this ruling," Bernard said. "They just don't know it yet. And if the pipes eventually collapse the street would have to be dug up which could cost the homeowner twenty thousand dollars or more. The good news," he added, "is your pipe is still in pretty good shape. But we'll have to auger it again. The camera picked up tissue snagged on the roots."

This was going from bad to worse. "But you just augured it!"

"Sure did, but that was just to get it flowing again. We just used a small brush. Now we have to do it again with a bigger brush."

This was Luke, the landscaper, all over again! Remove *all* the roots? Now *that* would have been a good deal, wouldn't it?

"Tell you what," Bernard said, throwing me a bone. "Let me call the town sewer department, and have them come out here. I understand they've got a chemical that we can shove in there to eradicate the roots permanently."

"Do the chemicals work?" (And the next question might have been, "And where do those chemicals go?")

"No one knows. The town won't pay for the camera to go back in and check. For that matter," Bernard confided, "I'm not a hundred percent sure that bylaw I was told about was passed. What I do know is they've hired a new supervisor and his mandate is to save costs."

This is great, I thought, a bylaw that at best was sneakily passed, and at worse was a complete abdication of the town's infrastructure obligation to its tax paying residents; or a bylaw that wasn't passed, but is being fabricated to pass the cost onto the homeowners. I don't know which is worse. (I could see the class dutifully taking notes.)

I filled Connie in on my discussions. "You've got to be kidding me!" she said. "Since when did I own the pipe under Banff Avenue? If that's the case I'm erecting a toll booth over it to pay for this fiasco." (Thanks to me she was turning more American every day. Now if only she could convince everyone else in town to block traffic, the conversion would be complete!)

Bernard called back five days later. "The town folks and I met and I showed them where the problem was."

"So are they going to pay for it?"

"No."

"Why not? The bylaw?"

"Nope, they didn't mention that. They're not going to pay for it because they say the roots are coming from your trees."

"Our trees? So in other words, if the trees were on town property, of which there are hundreds, causing a blockage inside the home-owner's property line, then they would pay for it?"

Bernard snickered quietly again. "They suggested you could cut down your trees."

"There are two problems with that. They are not our trees. Home-owners lease the land from Parks Canada and can neither cut nor plant any trees without their permission. And since this is a town-wide problem, are they seriously suggesting we cut down all the trees in Banff, a national heritage site?"

Bernard was silent.

I called another plumber, an expert on the town's pipes. "This has nothing to do with tree roots," he said. "Roots are drawn to moisture, and the roots wouldn't be inside the pipes unless moisture was seeping out from cracks in the pipe. The pipes are old and probably made of clay, and it makes sense they'd be more damaged under the street than under your lawn. They need to be replaced."

"And to this day, children, the town has not resolved this issue. Why? Because as long as they do nothing, when the sewer backs up it will remain Connie's problem, a problem she will have to finan-cially address immediately, no matter who is responsible. So children what have we learned from this civics lesson today?"

A little girl waved her hand. "That possession is not nine tenths of the law?"

"No, that we need to redirect the pipes into the homes of the city council!"

The children laughed and shouted, and vowed to tell everyone what a wonderful lecture they had heard, that living in a small town, a resort town, had its ins and outs, its ups and downs, but until *your* problem becomes *their* problem the system can become hopelessly clogged.

*All stories deserve an ending. After many worrisome months of town inaction we contacted the local paper. The town suddenly took an interest. They augured the pipe themselves. The pipe broke. Now they had to fix it. They did. All were happy in the end . . . really, we were.

Chapter 26

"Mush!"

The Norwegians invented skiing. And in the early 1900s when Banff locals peered out over their snow shoes at these strangers careening downhill on wooden sticks, they frankly thought they were crazy.

And maybe they were! Norway's hero, remember, is Thor Heyerdahl who in 1947 built a balsa-wood raft, pushed it into the waters off Peru . . . and sat there, in suicidal hopes of proving that Peruvians drifted 8,000 kilometers and first colonized the Polynesian Islands fifteen hundred years earlier.

But I digress. The fact is (after much anthropological research) only one thing separated man from ape, and it isn't the joy of swinging from a tree limb (just look at those Olympians on the uneven bars). No, it's the desire to slide downhill on our bums. Gazing through the leaves, anxiously, it was this, and this alone, that brought our species down from the trees. And to the bafflement of less intelligent species we've been breaking arms, legs, and collarbones doing it ever since.

I arrived back in Banff with the town covered in snow, and found myself staring at a strange pair of skis in the Whyte Museum. Made of hard, heavy wood they stood over seven feet tall. But what fascinated me was a strip of animal skin, animal skin with fur, tied snugly to the back of the skis.

"What's that for?" I asked Connie.

"That's how they climbed up the slopes. The hair lies flat one way and then stands up the other way to keep them from sliding backwards."

Forget today's fog-free goggles and the modern day skis and bindings. What they didn't have in the beginning, and this is important, was a ride up the mountain. Not a gondola, not a chairlift, not a mechanized rope pull, not even a hand-over-hand pulley (even the Chinese drew a line helping on this one*). Instead, in equal measures of pain and pleasure, they stepped up the slopes.

But it was the invention of the motorized rope pull (replacing, I might add, one mine owner's Sunday generosity, carting people up in ore buckets) that launched skiing as a commercial enterprise. With the giddy realization that people would pay for the tow, one of the first ski cabins was constructed in 1928 on Norquay Mountain, where forest fires and logging had helped carve out the slopes.

Other ski lodges, some only accessible by horseback or dog sled, were soon erected. Today they're called back country lodges and are popular destinations for summertime hikers. But these same rustic

---

*As noted in Rob Alexander's *History of Canmore,* once the railway was completed the Chinese comprised one of the largest ethnic minorities in Bow Valley. And they were quickly employed by the coal mines where they were often assigned to the bottom of the mine shafts, the most dangerous site to work. Alexander points out that the mine owners registered the Chinese by number. Records show that nineteen-year-old Lee Chong, who "worked at the picking table sorting rock and debris, was listed as Chinaman No. 39." Treated like children, the Chinese miners, in a back-handed compliment, were praised for being honest, hard working, cheap labor.

One hundred years later, though Canada is multi-cultured, observers might say that the government is still uncomfortable with a mixed race identity, as evidenced by the recent removal of an Asian looking woman from the back of Canada's $100 bill in favor of a white, Anglo-Saxon image.

lodges, expensively quaint, were the harbingers of Banff's modern-day ski resorts, which have made Banff a year-round tourist destination.

But for Connie and most Banff B&B owners, the summer, not the winter, is the busy season. "No Vacancy" signs are hung while Connie returns to teaching and others return to their regular jobs, leaving the hotels to happily accommodate the skiers.

I awoke early and looked out the window. Smoke from the hotel across the street was spiraling upward, instead of laying flat as it had the past week, a sign that today, a sunny Saturday, wasn't going to be as cold. In fact, by comparison, it was going to be downright warm. The winter had already seen a few days of forty degrees below zero, and at forty below, Fahrenheit and Celsius temperatures are the same.

I watched a woman stroll down the sidewalk, a local I determined, her hair blonder in the sun. How do you tell a local from a tourist? Easy. The local strides down the street with a sense of purpose.

But I'm not sure anyone in Banff, no matter how long they've lived here, truly feels like a local . . . unless being a local feels like you're on the outside looking in. The thing is, Banff has a plethora of niches, enthusiasts that would make the most long-standing resident wonder, "Who *are* those people?"

There are the summer athletes poling along the road on roller blades or biking furiously up steep grades. There are the "night people," a whole segment that parties all night and sleeps half the day. There are the rock climbers, mountaineers, naturalists, and bio-conservationists. Cowboys, the real deal, wander into town, and wonder, like Connie and me, why no one invited them to join their curling team.

It's weird and wonderful, and somewhat disconcerting to see so many people passionately pursuing their interests right before your eyes. It makes me ponder if any of them sneak a peak at Connie

serenely planting her red geraniums in the yard of her bed and breakfast, and wonder if that's what it is to be a local. But winter had settled in, narrowing everyone's passions, making us all feel as though
somehow we belonged.

"Connie," I hollered. "Let's see if we can find some remnants from
the old town of Anthracite!"

Before there was Banff, before there was much of anything in
Bow Valley, a tiny mining town aptly named Anthracite had been
erected along the Cascade River. Anthracite was known as a high
quality coal which propels much heat but little flame and smoke.
Founded in 1883 the town had seven saloons, a brothel, two hotels,
three general stores, a bakery, a church, and a pool hall. But three
massive floods and the price of its expensive coal doomed the small
town to failure, and it was officially abandoned in 1904.

All Connie and I knew was that it was three kilometers east of
Banff, and there might be a few artifacts remaining. An old photo
with identifiable cliffs in the background gave us a clue to its location.

We crunched along an abandoned snow packed road, keeping the
cliffs in sight, until we trudged down a steep incline, and there it was,
the remains of an old bridge that once led into town. We searched
along the river, but all we could see were the depressions in the ground
where houses once stood. That was all that was left . . . except for one
thing. Patches of wild rhubarb sprouted above the snow, originally
imported by the townspeople over a hundred years ago.

We began our walk back, a more relaxed time for hiking in the
Rockies. The bears were now hibernating, and *rutting* season for the
bull elk had ended (I hate that word. It sounds so . . . animalistic.),
so even the elk were less dangerous.

That left only the cougar, also known as a mountain lion, as
nature's chief predator. But cougars were rarely seen, preferring to
stay hidden from sight, and other than a cross country skier who
was attacked and killed by a cougar a decade ago, there had been

few encounters reported. There was nothing to fear. Unless, of course, it was agitated. Connie and I stared at the track in the snow. It came out of the woods, and then followed the road ahead of us. With four round toes, and no claw marks, it clearly belonged to the cat family. And with each step a drop of red blood splattered in the snow from a cut on the cat's right paw.

Two inches in diameter, with about a one foot stride, the foot print was too small to be a cougar. It was also too small to be a lynx, whose fur covered pad, despite its diminutive size, is larger than a mountain lion's. It had to be a bobcat. Unless, UNLESS it was a young cougar limping home to its mother.

A cougar can weigh up to two hundred pounds. Stretching three meters long, with speed and stealth, its incisors can quickly cut its prey's spinal cord. Thankfully, like I said, it's rarely seen.

But should you come face-to-face with one here's what you're supposed to do. Look bigger than you are. And WHATEVER YOU DO don't take your eyes off it. (Who the hell would? "Hey hon, look at those clouds over there. You think it might rain today?")

A man who survived a swat from one described it as "like being hit in the head with a 2x4 with four nails on the end of it." (Imagine in one lifetime being attacked by a cougar *and* being hit in the head by a 2x4 with four nails on the end of it!)

Connie and I had no choice but to follow the bloody trail. Whatever it was it was wounded, and neither of us was disappointed to eventually see the tracks disappear into the woods.

———

I had noticed a sign posted on the bulletin board at the local library. "Reading partners wanted to help with English." The flyer went on to explain no experience was needed. Winter workers came to Banff from around the globe, and they needed help with English, and filling out forms and applications. I volunteered.

I was assigned to a man in his twenties from the western side of New Brunswick where French is often spoken. He was working as a salad bar chef. He was kind and appreciative, and he also had a nervous demeanor. But this time, our third session together, he was particularly anxious. He'd had a confrontation with a waiter and feared his job was at risk. It didn't sound like a fireable offense, but that didn't matter. What mattered was in the moment he was upset . . . and that wasn't going to help him think clearly.

"I've got an idea," I said. "Instead of sitting here in the library reading newspaper articles let's go for a drive and read information signs placed at various view points?"

I had noticed that nature for me had a calming effect, and I was curious what impact it would have on him. We drove to Johnson Lake and read a placard on loons and wildlife. Then we turned up the Bow Valley Parkway and read about glaciers and animal migrations. Each time, I lingered, commenting on the trees and peaks in the distance, or a bird that had just landed on a limb. It was amazing. In a short time his breathing steadied, his voice grew softer, and there was hardly a sign he'd been troubled.

So what exactly was it that had such a tranquilizing effect? Some say it's the passage of time. The Rockies have been here for millions of years and will be here long after we're gone. Others say it's the size and space of the mountains. Diminished by such immensity how significant can our problems be? Still others have postulated that it's more primitive than that . . . perhaps when it comes to nature, we're just quietly going home.

All so true. But I have rallied in my quest for an answer around the immortal words of a third grader Connie had coincidentally taken on a field trip.

"Are you having fun?"

"It beats the heck out of sitting in a classroom."

Balanced atop a skateboard a young man in a winter hat careened by on Beaver Street. He went by in a blur, grasping a long rope he'd harnessed to his pet Husky.

"How do you stop?" I shouted.

"I don't," he hollered back. "I just jump off!"

Only in Banff, I thought, I love this town.

Connie joined me outside, dressed warmly in her scarf and jacket.

"What are you smiling about?"

"Nothing," I replied. "Just one man's approach to life."

We walked across the street, with no real destination in mind, and glanced back at the bed and breakfast. Its red cedar siding and bare trees looked inviting in the surrounding snow.

"It won't be long now," Connie said.

"Until what?"

"Until we take down the 'No Vacancy' sign."

"And then?"

Connie smiled. "We start all over again."

Author's Note

Though the events in the book are true to the best of my recollection, and historical portions are recorded as chronicled, any attempt by the reader to decipher an accurate narrative timeline (which I've creatively expanded and contracted) will leave you as baffled as me.

My thanks to my editor, Lori Crockett, who deftly polished the manuscript, and to Connie Beatson, the first and last reader prior to publication, the finest reviewer a writer could hope to have. All shortcomings are solely mine.

Illustration and Photo Credits

Front cover – *painting of Banff Avenue B&B* – Jamie Frazer, British Columbia

Map – Susan Beaupre – Leesburg, Virginia

Front cover – *Moraine Lake* – unknown

Inside covers – *Bow Lake* – Lawrence Carter, Banff, Alberta
                           Highline Magazine award-winning photo

Back cover – *Two Jack Lake* – Amrita Choudhury, Montreal,

Title page – *Rundle Mountain, Vermillion Lakes*,
                  Denise Giguére, Montreal

Map page – *Ten Peaks, Larch Valley*, Denise Giguére, Montreal

Chapter Three – *Bill Peyto* – unknown

Chapter Nine – *Hermit's cabin* – Ashlee Arlington, Australia

Chapter Twenty Three – *elk*, Denise Giguére, Montreal

Chapter Twenty Four – *Johnson Lake*, Denise Giguére, Montreal

Chapter Twenty Six – *Moon over Banff*, Amrita Choudhury, Montreal

About the author – *Connie and Jamie*, Kyle Beatson, Canmore, Alberta

FINALIST
MARFIELD PRIZE
NATIONAL AWARD FOR ARTS WRITING
2010

THE
ADVANCE
MAN

❀

*A Journey Into
the World of the Circus*

JAMIE MACVICAR

"A fascinating glimpse into the world of live-event marketing. With the book's well-timed humor and pacing, the reader is swept along."

- *SanFrancisco Book Review*

"*The Advance Man* nails it! The arc of the character is rich. The writing is superb, and the subject matter is as good as it gets."

- Bill Powell, VP of Marketing
Feld Entertainment

"THE GOLDEN AGE OF THE CIRCUS had passed but under Irvin Feld, the ruthless, unpredictable, super salesman, another golden age of promotion had just begun."

And so begins the extraordinary tale of *The Advance Man*. It's a history, a love story, and a tale of self-discovery. And as much, it's a captivating inside look at the largest traveling entertainment conglomerate on the globe, Ringling Bros. and Barnum & Bailey Circus.

www.Amazon.com

BEAR MANOR MEDIA
ALBANY, GEORGIA

• *Publishers of Quality Entertainment Biographies* •

Bibliography

Ackerman, Andrew. *The Handbook of the Canadian Rockies*. Department of Environmental Studies

Alexander, Rob. *The History of Canmore*. Banff: Summerthought Publishing, 2010

Appleby, Edna. *Canmore, The Story of an Era*. Canmore, 1975

Armstrong, Christopher. Evander, Matthew. Nelles, H.V. *The River Returns: An Environmental History of the Bow*. Montreal: McGill-Queen's University Press, 2009

Bear 71, National Film Board of Canada, Web Documentary by Leanne Allison and Jeremy Mendes.

Brooks, David. *New York Times*. Article on blue collar perspectives. 2007 Ref., Chapter five—manipulators . . . impacting their lives . . . where character counts.

Conaty, Gerald. Betenia, Daryl. Mastin, Catharine. *The Bow: Living With a River*. Glenbow Museum, 2004

DiManno, Corrie. *Year of the Forest*. Banff: *Crag and Canyon*, 2011

Foubert, Tanya. *Drug Courier Spared Jail Time*. Banff: *Rocky Mountain Outlook*, 2011

Gadd, Ben. *Bankhead: The Twenty Year Town*. Banff: The Friends of Banff National Park, 1989

Gadd, Ben. *Geology of the Canadian Rockies and Columbia Mountains*. Notes on lecture, 2008

Halfpenny, James. *Scats and Tracks of the Rocky Mountains*. Guilford, Connecticut: The Globe Pequot Press, 1998

Hart, E.J. *Ain't it Hell*. Banff: Summerthought Publishing, 1995

Hart, E.J. *Diamond Hitch*. Banff: EJH Literary Enterprises Ltd., 1999

Hart, E.J. *The Place of Bows*. Banff: Summerthought Ltd., 1979

Hempstead, Andrew. *Exploring the History of Banff*. Banff: Summerthought Publishing, 2012

Hopper, Tristin. *Dreams and Difficulty*. Toronto: *National Post*, 2012

Hutchings, Sebastian.*Banff: History, Attractions, and Activities*. Canmore: Altitude Publishing Ltd., 2002

Kelly, John. *John Kelley's Washington*. Washington D.C.: *The Washington Post*, 2012

Lynch, Wayne. *Mountain Bears*. Calgary: Fifth House Ltd., 1999

Mittelstadt, David. *Calgary Goes Skiing*. Surrey: Rocky Mountain Books, 2005

Patton, Brien. *Tales from the Canadian Rockies*. Edmonton: Hurtig Publishers, 1984

Sandford, R.W. *The Book of Banff*. Banff: The Friends of Banff National Park, 1994

Sandford, R.W. *Seeing and Believing*. The International Year of Mountains, 2002

Whyte Museum, Banff, Alberta. 2013 Exhibit—and Parks Canada

About the Author

JAMIE MACVICAR is the author of *The Advance Man: A Journey Into the World of the Circus*, which was awarded Finalist honors for the Marfield Prize - National Award for Arts Writing. He is the co-author of *Crossed Pens*. His short stories and feature articles have been widely published. jmacvicar@cox.net